Endorsements for

We read it and we loved it!

Sara and Francis Fontana have been a great inspiration and support for us as a couple. They have also positively influenced us in what God has called us to do: To do our part to help others build better marriages and better families. We first met Sara and Francis when we shared our pastoral work at St. Paul in Nassau Bay, Texas. They had recently published the first edition of their book *Bullseye Marriage*. We read it and we loved it! We had talked about collaborating in a project, but we never imagined that it would be in the adaptation of their book to reach the Spanish speaking community. *Bullseye Marriage* has been a blessing for our marriage, our family and for many others. Sara and Francis have a fresh and very accurate message based on their own experience of living an intense and intentional marriage. We are confident that this will continue to be a blessing that will help many, many couples.

Jose Juan and Alba Iris Valdez

The Spanish adaptation of the book is <u>Anotando Gol en tu Matrimonio</u> and can be found on Amazon or on the Valdez' webpage <u>www.seranlosdosuno.com</u>

An invitation to grow in commitment and love for one another

I have known Francis and Sara Fontana and their family for over 30 years. They have always been an inspiration to me and, through the years, have modeled and taught me a great deal in regards to the Sacrament of Matrimony, married life, and family. For this, I am most grateful. *Bullseye Marriage* is an invitation for couples to grow in their commitment and love for one another. And, it is a methodology of how to daily grow into this commitment and love. Thank you, Francis and Sara, for sharing your commitment with us.

Rev. James Burkart, Pastor
Christ the Good Shepherd Catholic Community
Spring, Texas

Dec. 2020

BULLSEYE MARRIAGE

Intentionally
Targeting

a

Sacramental
Relationship

To Michael (JOP)

We are praying for you

J. Cristina!

Sara Fontana

By
Sara and Francis Fontana

Sara and Francis Fontana

bullseyemarriage@yahoo.com

ISBN: 978-151227460

Cover Design and illustrations by Peter Fontana

To our parents
Ralph and Joy Guidroz
&
Tony and Evelyn
Fontana

ACKNOWLEDGEMENTS

To all those who encouraged us to write a book on marriage, we want to say a profound and deep felt thank you. The process of writing has been a wonderful time of reflection and discussion on our marriage. It has caused us to seek out websites and books of those who have far more expertise than we do when it comes to strengthening marriages. It has also caused us to have incredible discussions with our children.

We are so grateful to our children and the insight they provided in the writing of this book. Our favorite chapter is the one they wrote. Our son, Peter, provided the cover, all the graphics and provided his technical and computer knowledge through the whole writing process.

We want to thank Heidi Clark and Criss Butler who spent time editing the manuscript. We also want to acknowledge Fr. Dominic Pistone who provided input as well as Winnie Honeywell, Anne Grizzle, Dr. David Thomas and Kim Noto.

We would be remiss to not acknowledge all of our siblings and our parents. Sara's parents, many of our siblings, nieces and nephews read copies and encouraged us in the writing process. We want to say a special thank you to Francis' brother and our sister-in-law, Dr. Robert and Lori Fontana, whose work with Catholic Life Ministries and their example through the years has both challenged and inspired us.

Our hope is that this writing and the concept of shooting for a Bullseye in your marriage will challenge and inspire you as well as strengthen you in your resolve to intentionally target a sacramental relationship.

BULLSEYE MARRIAGE:

Intentionally Targeting a Sacramental Relationship

TABLE OF CONTENTS

FOREWORD:
By Peter Fontana

Most days, Mom wakes up at around five in the morning, partly because she fell asleep mid-sentence while enlightening you about her most recent philosophy on life at around nine the evening before, but mostly because she cherishes the stillness and clarity that come in the early morning twilight. I was usually the first to stumble downstairs because, much to my dismay, my classes started earlier than my three siblings. She would inevitably look up from her favorite chair by the fireplace with an aromatic cup of English breakfast tea, an open Bible, and her day planner laid out in front of her, flash a smile that was undeniable evidence that she was much more awake than should be legal at that hour of the morning, and offer a chipper "Good Morning!" at a volume that seemed to assault my less than alert ears. Mom had already prayed through her day to work out the kinks of what *she* wanted to get done and what *God* actually had in store for her, and then she had moved on and done the same for each of us in the house…including Dad.

Dad, on the other hand, actually *enjoys* sleep. He gets

out of bed much like the rest of us with little more than coffee on his mind, good strong Community Coffee dark roast, nonetheless. However, as soon as he shows signs of stirring, one to two hours after her, Mom, who mind you has already worked out his schedule and thought through all of the causes and effects of any decisions that have to be made through the entire day, assaults the poor man with a beautifully rehearsed presentation of her thoughts on each major point on the day's schedule and starts asking questions with seemingly zero connection ("do you have the folding chairs in your car?"... "Um... yes?" Mom's deductions, "that means we can take his car to the soccer game and he probably doesn't want to go to the store today, but he will want to cook... etc.). Dad, undeterred, continues pouring his cup of coffee and sits down while letting my mother finish her barrage.

He then answers with something similar to, "Sara, I really want to hear all of this, can we talk about it in 15 minutes?" An accepting smile of resignation would form on my Mothers face, as she would nod her consent. Dad knows that Mom is the reason he gets anything done on any given day. And Mom knows that Dad's brain does not process until coffee is consumed; so if she continues, she will get a call in about an hour asking what the schedule is for the day.

The humor I witnessed in many versions of this scene through the years never took away from the truth that it presented to me as an adolescent growing up. To me, this little act spelled out security and love. It meant that Dad and Mom loved each other and knew what the word "love" meant. It meant that they were committed to each other and committed to accepting the other person and doing whatever it took to make their love work regardless of the cost. It meant that I had a Mom and a Dad who were going to be *married* and living lives of fulfillment for as long as they were on earth together.

What I learned from Mom and Dad was that marriage does not work like a well-oiled machine - so, don't expect it to. It usually works more like that old Honda weed eater my Dad has in the garage. It needs about an hour of work for every half hour of weed eating you want to do. Sometimes the work is frustrating, sometimes it is hilarious, but it always takes some patience, some care and a little elbow grease. In the end, though, it's more about time you spend together working on it; it is more about the journey.

You see, the beauty about Mom and Dad is that they don't have a Ph.D. in marriage counseling and a million dollar book deal. The beauty is that they are that typical couple you meet at your kid's soccer game- a guy who likes the Saints and would fish all day if he could and a girl who loves to chat and will know your entire life's story if you sit down to tea with her for fifteen minutes. They are the average couple who really wanted to get it right, and because of that they came away with an extraordinary marriage relationship and family. After twenty-nine years my Mom still sits on my Dad's lap to watch movies. They have the marriage that keeps getting better.

My wife, Kristin, and I just celebrated our first 18 months of marriage. We have a beautiful six-month-old daughter. When we said "I do," a year and a half ago, we said it in full knowledge of what we were getting into and in full confidence that our sacrament would end in "death do us part." Mom and Dad instilled in Kristin and me the tools we needed to enter into a marriage that has started out great and is only getting better.

What follows in these pages is not a "12 Step Program to a Great Marriage!" written by a guy who wants to sell books. What follows is a trailhead. If you start walking down the trail my parents have laid out, as my wife and I have, you begin to discover the true freedom that is marriage. Men will discover marriage as the epic adventure where they truly are the hero who must be at once the strong protector of their clan and the passionate lover of their wife. Women discover that they are the maiden their man is defending as well as the counselor who holds the ship on course. It is when you begin walking and discovering the adventure together that marriage starts to work.

Yes, Mom & Dad have hit the Bullseye, and they can teach you how to hit it as well. But what you will unearth as you set out on this trail, is that just hitting the Bullseye is not where the treasure lies; it is waking every morning knowing that you get another day to hit or miss the target. Either way, you're going to keep shooting until you start to strike the Bullseye more than you miss it.

My parents live a life that is truly fulfilled through walking the day-to-day journey living out of the sacrament of marriage. They are proof that doing the work to hit the Bullseye is worth it... a hundred times over. It shines through in their very countenance whether their current emotion is joy, sadness, or frustration. I, with my wife, invite you to start shooting...

(Written in 2010)

CHAPTER ONE:
Why Bullseye Marriage…

Work on your marriage and your marriage will work.

Dr. Robert Fontana

Sara tells the story…

We walked into Viking Archery and immediately encountered a water fountain and a big brown bear that graced the room. The bear hovered, frozen in taxidermic time, over a set of chairs in the midst of many arrow selections and hunting paraphernalia. Through an opening in the wall immediately to our left, we saw two men and a woman sitting behind a counter, watching TV. They looked up when we walked in.

One of them asked, "Can we help you?" I said, "I called about coming in and using your indoor archery place." The woman responded, "Have you ever shot arrows before?" Francis told her he had taught archery in the past. I told her that years ago I had taught archery at a day camp, but that was only because they did not have anyone else to teach it. It was not because I knew anything about it.

As we spoke, we walked into the room with the counter as one of the men fired questions at me:

"Are you right-handed or left-handed?"

"Mostly right, but I shoot pool left-handed."

"Which hand do you throw a ball with?"

"Normally, my right hand."

"Are you right-eye dominant or left-eye dominant?"

"I have no idea."

"Can you see the targets?" he asked, as he pointed through a large open window behind the counter that provided access to the indoor archery range.

"Yes."

"Point to the center of one with both eyes open." I obediently pointed at the target. He instructed, "Now close your right eye." I followed his direction and the target looked like it moved to the right. He told me to close only my left eye. I said, "Now the target is on the left." The man started laughing and the woman spoke up. "Take both of your hands and put them together leaving a triangle opening." She demonstrated this action and looked at me through the opening in her hands. I held up my hands in the same manner and looked at her with both eyes through the triangle opening in my hands. She said, "Close your left eye."

"I can still see you."

"Open your left eye and close your right eye."

"I can't see you through the opening anymore."

"You are right-eye dominant."

The man, who had fired all the questions at me, walked into the indoor archery range and Francis and I followed him to a section of the room where bows were hanging. He took one down, strung it and handed it to me. "See if you can pull that." He did the same with Francis with a different bow. The bows looked the same but the tightness of the string was based on our strength to pull it back. Both Francis and I were right-eye dominant so he selected a bow that assisted us in shooting effectively with our right eye.

He handed us several arrows each and directed us to one of the designated shooting areas. There were several people already shooting. The man said that when everyone was finished shooting, someone would say, "pull," and that would mean everyone stops shooting so they can go pull the arrows from the target. He asked us if we wanted to shoot at the existing target or if we wanted a new one. Both Francis and I replied that we wanted a new one. He went and got us two new targets and when someone said, "pull," we walked down and he showed us how to put up our new target.

When we walked back to the shooting area, both Francis and the man gave me some lessons on how to stand and how to set the arrow. The first arrow I shot did not make it to the target. There was a gentleman in the next shooting space who watched me shoot. He mentioned he was an instructor and asked if I would like a few tips. I said "Of course. He proceeded to give me tips on how to stand: "Your body should make a perfect upright T formation. No leaning. Pull the arrow to your nose, rest your thumb underneath your chin, get the target in sight, let go and watch the arrow all the way through till it hits." I combined his instruction with what Francis and the other man had said and shot another arrow. This one actually hit the wall near the target!

For the next hour, Francis and I shot arrows at our targets. The instructor would interject other tips on improving our ability, which Francis and I incorporated into our shooting practice. Francis was much more consistent with hitting the target. I improved with practice. In the end, Francis had a target that had many hits with one in the bullseye area. I had as many arrows hit the wall around the target as on the target, but I did get two in the bullseye area!

We discovered that we had used muscles that we had not used on a regular basis. As we got tired and those muscles got a little sore, it was harder to stay accurate. We were often off the target during that time. We also found that there were some tools that helped with easing the hurt such as covers that protected the fingers from hurting each time you pulled the bow back and arm bands that eased the muscles.

Both Francis and I had a desire to get it right in the center of the bullseye area. Even though we did not do it in that round, we had a great time trying! We had gone to practice archery to see if there were some good analogies between archery and shooting for a great marital relationship. We had been writing a book on relationships and had conducted marriage conferences under an earlier title *A Bridge to Love: Intentionally Building a Great Marriage.*

How we use the story...

The Bridge title came out of a discussion we had with a friend who had insisted that we should write a book on marriage. He, earlier in his life, had the opportunity to meet Viktor Frankl, the well known psychiatrist who wrote *Man's Search for Meaning.* One of the things that Frankl encouraged our friend to do was to take a paper and on the right side of the paper write down all the things he wanted to accomplish in life. On the left side of the paper, Frankl instructed our friend to write down where he was currently. The last step was to draw a bridge from the left side of the paper, where he was now, to the right side of the paper, where he wanted to be. "Then," Viktor Frankl told our friend, "work toward building a bridge in your life that gets you from where you are now to where you want to be."

Viktor Frankl's instruction to our friend translated in our mind to intentionally building a great marriage. We used the analogy of the bridge in the early stages of writing and in the marriage conferences we conducted. But as we presented it at the earlier marriage conferences the bridge analogy kept falling short. It did not quite get us to what we were shooting for in writing the book and conducting the marriage conferences. The purpose of Viktor Frankl's exercise was to get our friend to focus on what he was aiming for in life, not the building of the bridge. The building of the bridge was the skills and experiences and knowledge that he would need to get him to where he wanted to go. The bridge is incredibly important, but it is not what we are aiming for when we set out to go somewhere; it is a way to get us there.

It was the word "aim" that moved us to focus on the analogy of the Bullseye. When we discuss our marriage and what we are aiming at we always conclude that what we want is a great relationship. There are many tools, books, and experiences that assist us in getting where we want to go, but to be effective we need to keep in mind what we are shooting for in our marriage. The archery analogy began to form in our minds. We changed the title to *Bullseye Marriage: Intentionally Targeting a Great Relationship.*

So after our practice run at Viking Archery we went to dinner to see if there were some effective analogies in what we had just experienced and in shooting for a great relationship in marriage. The chapters of the book came directly out of that experience:

Chapter Two: What's your Bullseye?

Unless you have a clear vision of what you are shooting for and where the target is, you will be hard pressed to even know where to aim. This chapter provides you a process we call a "sensory brainstorm" as you work toward creating a clear vision of what a Bullseye marriage would like for you. If you read this as a couple this chapter is an opportunity to decide if you are shooting at an "existing target" or is it time to freshen it up and create a new one that you both can agree on.

Chapter Three: What's your Experience?

The question behind this question is the important one. What is your history with relationships? What was your parents' relationship like? What is your life story? What experience, both good and bad, have you had with earlier relationships? This chapter offers a Masterpiece Timeline Activity for you to do as a couple.

Chapter Four: Are you right handed or left handed?

Before Sara could even pick up a bow and arrow she had to know whether she was right handed or left handed, right-eye dominant or left-eye dominant. The only person one can control in any relationship is oneself. If you are in a relationship, or planning to enter one, it's important to be in touch with yourself. It helps to have someone assist in this matter and to get advice and ideas from different books and sources. It took two people providing different ideas to help Sara in learning that she was right-eye dominant. This chapter offers ways and resources to assist you in getting to know yourself better. It's important to realize as you read this chapter that no person is stagnant; our life experiences and knowledge shape our philosophy and outlook. To know yourself is a lifetime process.

Chapter Five: Men & Women shoot differently.

The man, who strung our bows, strung them differently. He strung them based on our strength. Each person in a relationship brings different strengths. Basic archery has skills that everyone can use, but men and women will bring, even to archery, their own approach and strength. Chapter Five delves into the different needs of men and women. The chapter challenges both parties in the relationship to listen and learn from one another and work toward a mutual relationship that utilizes the strengths of both.

Chapter Six: What happens when you get tired?

When we got tired our arrows were less accurate. In 90 minutes, we shot between 125-150 arrows and only 3 hit the bullseye. Many hit the target and a number completely missed. Just like marriage. Whatever the picture in your mind of the perfect relationship, it is rarely met. That doesn't mean you quit trying. Marriages work when you work on the marriage. To set aside a marriage because you are tired prevents you from ever experiencing the joy of hitting a bullseye. Instead, when you are tired learn to take what we call "tower time."

Chapter Seven: Tips for Hitting the Bullseye

Just as there are different tools that you can use in archery to make practice less painful and more fun; there are tools and tips that help make the work of marriage less hurtful and more enjoyable. With that in mind this Chapter gives quick tips and ideas.

Chapter Eight:
Those Who Benefit from a Bullseye Marriage

A marriage is not just between two people. The two are connected to their family of origin, their friends, to children who come forth from them and more. When a couple struggles, it affects the whole system. When a couple thrives it also affects the whole system. This chapter recognizes that no marriage is perfect, but research proves that there are no losers when a couple continues to work on their marriage. In this chapter we give our children an opportunity to say how they have benefited from our continuing to work on our marriage.

Chapter Nine: Resources

This chapter is filled with books and websites that assist you in working on your Bullseye Marriage. It also refers to the Catholic Catechism and has a listing of specific teachings on marriage. We have even put together a *"History of Marriage in a Nutshell"*.

Francis takes aim....

Sara and I married on August 8, 1981. During the first stage of our marriage we were both Youth Ministers and I also taught theology at a Catholic high school. In 1985, I started my financial service business with Primerica. Over the years, I have had the privilege to visit with thousands of couples and individuals. In visiting with these couples and single adults, I have witnessed a multitude of different relationships. Being a people person, I became interested in the story of their relationships: How did they meet? How long have they been married? Are their parents still married to each other? Are they actively involved in a faith community? If divorced, what was it that led to their separation/divorce? What was the catalyst for a successful relationship or a failed relationship? And on and on...

Since I have been in this business for the vast majority of the years we have been married, these one-on-one visits, mostly in the comforts of the couple's own home, have been my classroom for studying successful and unsuccessful relationships. I have made it my study over the years to learn from each of these relationships. In sharing these experiences with my wife, it has enabled us to learn from those who have been down the road of life further than we have and to build upon their successes and learn from their failures.

Two events led me to collaborating with Sara in writing a book on marriage. The first was our oldest son announcing his engagement to be married. Peter was born in 1986 and had witnessed the majority of the years of our marriage. On our 25th wedding anniversary he gave us two framed testimonies. A separate one to each of us of what he had learned through the years of observing our relationship with each other, with our children and with others. We share his words in Chapter 8. As I have witnessed his relationship with Kristin, his wife, I am convinced he has learned a great deal from Sara and I. He and Kristin have taken their relationship to a higher level than I would have ever dreamed of at such a young age.

The second event was the result of saying, "yes," to the Lord in a dream. I became involved in a men's retreat program called ACTS (Adoration, Community, Theology, Service). To make a long story short, I had a dream one night that I needed to direct the next men's ACTS Retreat, and there was someone I was supposed to meet. I agreed to be the director of the retreat and it turned out to be one of the most profound experiences of my life. On the weekend I met many men whose stories touched me deeply. There was one man whom I connected with in a special way, and I believe was the man from my dream. He was persistent in encouraging me to write the book. He wanted to have it all— a successful marriage, a great family, and a successful business. He was looking for those who were witness to that achievement. We had discussions that it is possible to achieve all three when two people are willing to continue to grow, change and work at their marriage.

I am grateful for the opportunity to work with Sara as we get in touch with our story and get in touch with those daily disciplines that move our marriage and our relationship to greatness. May these words help you get in touch with your own story and the process of becoming your best so that you can build a great relationship that will be your legacy.

Sara's Turn...

Francis and I met at St. Edmond's Church in Lafayette, Louisiana. Francis was youth minister to my parish youth group, which I never participated in while I was in high school. It wasn't until I graduated from high school that my mother, at a going away party for our assistant pastor, introduced me to him. I had decided during the summer that I wanted to be more involved in Church and possibly pursue a ministry career. I spoke to Francis about getting involved in the youth program and he asked if I would like to work with the Confirmation program. Thus began our friendship.

I'll never forget the day that we both realized that there was more than friendship between us. We had gone to meet some friends to go dancing. We walked in the door and I saw my friends on the right hand side and he saw his friends on the left hand side. We grabbed each other's hands to go to meet our friends and wound up pulling in the opposite direction. When we looked into each other's eyes, I realized there was a difference; there was something more than just friendship present in the touch of our hands. We kissed each other that night for the first time.

We began going to mass together and spending time in prayer together as well as going on dates. We discovered many similar interests. I loved our conversations and spending time with him. The first birthday gift he ever gave me was a Bible. In it he wrote a beautiful letter, "I pray that the Lord, with His goodness, will strengthen us and draw us closer together...I really feel that the Lord holds something very special for us."

That Bible and those words are a symbol of the strength of our relationship. It is founded on God and in a strong belief that God does strengthen us, draws us closer together and continuously has something special in mind for us. That thought permeated the space between us when I moved to Houston, Texas. I dated other people and pursued my college degree at University of St. Thomas. Francis and I continued to talk and see each other when he could make the trip to Houston or I could get to Lafayette. A year after he moved to Houston for a youth ministry position, we were engaged to be married.

We went through Engaged Encounter, Sponsor Couple and attended Natural Family Planning classes. Our approach for preparing for the Sacrament of Marriage was similar to a seminarian preparing for the Sacrament of Holy Orders in the Catholic Church. We spent time in prayer, study, spiritual direction, and discernment of our vocation. Our year of engagement was our final discernment in preparing for final vows. We continued to believe that God would strengthen us and draw us closer together or the process would show us we were not to be married. On August 8, 1981 we exchanged marriage vows under the same roof where we had met.

Our Catholic background, our relationship with Jesus and the depth of our faith, is central to our own definition of what a Bullseye Marriage looks like to us. Each of the chapters is designed to help you get in touch with your own background, belief system and life experiences which will be part of how you define what a Bullseye Marriage looks like for you. Our assumption is that if you are reading this book you have a desire to aim at a relationship that is beyond ordinary. One tat is provides the fullness of life promised in the Gospels. Our hope is that our stories, words and exercises, joined with the other books you've read and your life experiences move you closer to the Bullseye in your marriage.

Closing...

In the midst of writing this book a good friend died. It was a sudden death. She was fine during Memorial Day weekend as two of her sons graduated, one from 8th grade and one from high school. Friday, Saturday and Sunday, she had a great celebration with her husband, their graduating sons, their other son, their daughter and the whole family. On Monday evening, she started feeling bad. Tuesday, she went to the doctor with flu-like symptoms. The doctor said it was a virus, not much they could do. Wednesday morning, she started having seizures. Her husband rushed her to the hospital; the virus had attacked her spinal cord and gone into her brain. Thursday, she was on life support. Friday she died. She was 49 years old.

All of us, who knew Rossana and Juan Barrios, were reeling with the suddenness of her death. Her wake and funeral were a testimony to a couple who for over 20 years had a Bullseye Marriage. They had defined what a great relationship was for them and lived out of that definition. Juan shared that definition at Rossana's funeral:

"Rossana allowed me, with the blessing of God, to be the head of our home, the leader of our family and the sustainer of our love. Many times we talked about how God had put us on earth to show others the strength of our marriage. She knew that God is the source of everything. Rossana and I lived, worked, grew, worshiped together as an example for others, putting our lives in God's hands. Rossana was given to me for this purpose. I was indeed privileged and honored by God. I am glad to say that our children originated within God's plan. They were sustained in a God-loving home. We did not let the mundane distractions of life stop us from encouraging, loving and supporting our children.

Rossana, the mother, did not just stop in our family. She did the same for all others. Her words of wisdom were strong and full of understanding. They were God- given. A daughter, a sister, a wife, a mother, a friend, she acted at all times with amazing unselfishness. She always had a genuine desire to give more of herself without any expectation of a return. She would tell me, "Juan, if someone comes to us for help in anything I want to say "yes" even if we may not be able to. I want you to support me on this." My awareness of her love for others grew with time. I started to include in my prayers that God give me the opportunity to follow and be like her. Now I have been given this opportunity fully. I have to lead within her example.

As a couple we worked on our marriage, our family, our love. Rossana knew that human life is precious, since it is God-given, and she also knew that eternal life is what we must strive for and she did. We should all rejoice now that Rossana has eternal life. God's plan is unfolding and going forward. I don't understand it but accept it. Rossana's purpose is part of God's plan. My heart hurts but is full of joy. Rossana has been the one to lead us again. God honors us all by having her with Him. Rossana, my love, Rossana, my wife, I thank God for choosing you for me."

Rossana and Juan had defined over time what their Bullseye was and worked toward developing the skills to hit the Bullseye in their marriage. Their Bullseye Marriage reflected their faith and their life experience. Rossana's funeral was only one of several that we have attended through the years of spouses who were part of a Bullseye Marriage.

It is all the more poignant when you are a witness to the end of a Bullseye Marriage because one of the partners has died. When you have been witness to a Bullseye Marriage or part of a Bullseye Marriage, you know that marriage really does work if you work at it. It's something you aim at on a daily basis. Some days you hit the Bullseye, some days you're excited that you hit the target at all, and then there are days when you are tired of trying and wonder if it is worth it to keep aiming at the Bullseye. It's remembering others who have been witnesses by their own lives together in their Bullseye Marriages that gives you the strength and belief it is worth it. We are forever grateful to the many couples in our life, like Juan and Rossana Barrios, who have been that witness to us and kept our belief in marriage alive.

Our hope for all who read this book is that it will sustain and strengthen you in your resolve to work at your marriage. Work has many definitions and connotations. In Webster Dictionary "work" is defined as "a sustained physical or mental effort to overcome obstacles and achieve an objective or result". Confucius says, "If you enjoy what you do, you'll never work another day in your life."

We believe that when we keep our focus on the great relationship we are trying to achieve – the work of marriage seems less like work and more centered on a purpose. It is very much like owning your own business doing something you love. You have a mission to fulfill and you are passionate about fulfilling that mission. As a business owner, that mission and your business are in your mind 24 hours a day. Yet, because you have a passion for it, it does not seem like work. You go about your day realizing what a privilege and honor it is to have the opportunity to spend the day doing what you love to do. There are still rough days, but you keep a better perspective during those days because you know happiness is right around the corner or tucked away in the midst of the struggle waiting to be uncovered.

Intentionally living out your marriage vows and ministering to each other's needs is the greatest gift you can give to your children and to all those around you. And, at the end of your life, out of all of your accomplishments, it will be one of the key areas of your life that people will remember the most. May the following few pages assist you in working on a Bullseye Marriage and intentionally targeting a sacramental relationship.

CHAPTER TWO: WHAT'S YOUR BULLSEYE?

Have you not read that from the beginning the Creator made them male and female and declared that 'for this reason a man shall leave his father and mother and be joined to his wife and the two shall become as one'? Thus they are no longer two but one flesh. Therefore, what God has joined together, no human being must separate.

Matthew 19:4 – 6
New American Bible

On your wedding day you most likely did not look your potential bride or groom in the eye and say, "I take you to be my spouse; I promise to TRY being married to you until it does not work anymore." No, more than likely you said something similar to the standard lines that are said in most marriage ceremonies, "I promise to be true to you in good times and in bad, in sickness and in health. I will love you and honor you all the days of my life." Your intention on that wedding day was that you were going to spend the rest of your life with the person you were marrying.

Spending your entire life with the same person is not an easy undertaking. But couples through the centuries have joined in marriage and stayed married to the same person all their lives. Marriage for life is one bullseye that couples are shooting for when they first begin their marriage. But is the objective of marriage to just stay married for life or is there something more? We believe there is something more.

We believe that through the centuries couples have desired more than just longevity in their marriage and that the Church, especially, has challenged couples to strive for more than just being lifelong companions. In fact, the Catholic Church designated marriage an official Sacrament in the 12th Century. It is the only one of the 7 Sacraments in the Roman Catholic Church where the persons who are receiving the Sacrament are actually authorized to be the minister of the Sacrament to one another. When a couple understands that they will be the ministers of a Sacrament of the Catholic Church, it raises the level of importance of the preparation. The focus is no longer just a wedding it is about a Sacramental Marriage. That is a marriage that is dedicated to the service of God.

The history of marriage is a fascinating study. Going into early Christian manuscripts located in the Bible and then following Church documents through the centuries, one can get a sense of how the understanding of the purpose of marriage has developed through the years. (See *History of Marriage in a Nutshell* in Chapter 9-Resource Section)

In 1994, the National Conference of Catholic Bishops issued out a wonderful document called *Follow the Way of Love*.

In it they challenged married couples to 'grow in mutuality:'

> *"Marriage is the partnership of a man and woman equal in dignity and value. This does not imply sameness in roles or expectations. There are important physical and psychological traits, which result in differing skills and perspectives. Nor does the equality of persons mean that two spouses will have identical gifts or character or roles.*
>
> *Rather, a couple who accepts their equality as sons and daughters in the Lord will honor and cherish one another. They will respect and value each other's gifts and uniqueness. They will "be subordinate to one another out of reverence for Christ." (Ephesians 5:21)*
>
> *For unlike other relationships, marriage is a vowed covenant with unique dimensions. In this partnership, mutual submission-not dominance by either partner-is the key to genuine joy. Our attitude should be the same as Jesus "who, though he was in the form of God, did not regard equality with God something to be grasped. Rather he emptied himself..." (Phil 2:6-7)*
>
> *Mutuality is really about sharing power and exercising responsibility for a purpose larger than ourselves. How household duties are distributed should follow from understanding what it takes to build a life together, as well as individual skills and interests you bring to your common life... True equality, understood*

as mutuality, is not measuring out tasks or maintaining an orderly schedule. It thrives at a much deeper level where the power of the Spirit resides. Here, the grace of the vowed life not only makes the shedding of willfulness possible, but also leads to a joyful willingness." (pp. 19 and 20)

When we got married in 1981 we agreed that divorce was not an option for us, but we also wanted a great relationship that worked toward mutuality. We both had different examples in our lives of married couples whom we felt had great relationships. Our observation of what made their relationships great was a starting point for discussion as we attempted to define for ourselves what a great relationship would be for us. It assisted us in defining the target we were shooting for and what a Bullseye Marriage would look like for us.

We realized that there was not another couple out there that had the same backgrounds as we did, the same upbringing, the same life experiences. We knew that we were not going to be able to find one couple who was exactly like us to pattern ourselves after. We had to pull from our observations of others along with the books, articles and documents that we had read, to define for ourselves what we were targeting.

We asked each of our parents to select one of the scripture readings for our wedding ceremony and to not only read it during the wedding but also tell us the gift they wanted us to receive from it. As Sara's mother, Joy Guidroz, offered so appropriately, "The gift I want to give you is to be free from any injunctions, any shoulds or oughts that I or anyone else has put on you. Look into your hearts for what is right for you. Communicate with one another what God is saying to you as a couple."

Through the years we have been gifted with many couples who have added to our understanding and definition of what a great relationship was to us. We would observe and discuss what the couples were reading, their use of television and movies, how they spoke to one another, their use of alcohol or drugs, the traditions they had, the activities they did together, even how they divided up household tasks. We would notice how they showed affection to one another, their holding hands or hugs or kisses given when they were leaving or returning. We participated in various couples' groups through our church and attended seminars to enrich our understanding of marriage. All these things helped us define what we were shooting for and affirmed the Bullseye Marriage that we targeted every day.

In creating the Bullseye Marriage Conferences we created a Sensory Brainstorm to help couples begin to write down observations of other couples they believed had a great relationship. During the conference we have the husbands brainstorm in one room and the wives brainstorm in the other. The important part of the exercise is to complete it separately and then get together to share answers.

SENSORY BRAINSTORM:

Take a moment and call to mind a married couple that you believe has a great relationship. (Maybe it's your own) Have the couple so clearly pictured in your brain that you are remembering the times that you have seen them together or heard them speak about their relationship. With that couple in mind, along with your experience of other couples and your own belief system, begin a "sensory brainstorm".

A "Sensory Brainstorm" is a quick way for you to get in touch with ways that a married couple uses their 5 senses in targeting a great relationship. We have listed the fives senses with starter thoughts to help prompt your brainstorming. Brainstorming is just listing ideas as they come to you about that particular topic. Let the ideas flow freely.

A MARRIED COUPLE WHO HAS A GREAT RELATIONSHIP....

    (watches, reads....)

    (Listens to, speaks to one another, says regularly...)

    (eats, mealtimes, use of drugs & alcohol,....)

    (has traditions, hygiene, activities they do together, etc......)

   (hugs, gives blessings, spends quality time, shows affection...)

We encourage you to make copies of the Sensory Brainstorm. Complete the information separately and then get together with your spouse to share answers. The Sensory Brainstorm can be a great starting point for discussion and brainstorming. There are no right or wrong answers, just observations and ideas that become starter discussions for you to begin to define what a Bullseye Marriage looks like for you.

You have to create your own target together. No two couples are alike so your ideas of what a Bullseye Marriage looks like and what to target will be different from other couples and may even be different from one another. It's important to realize, much of what you believe makes up a good marriage is based upon your history. The goal is to find the similarities and a common target that will be unique to you as a couple.

Choosing your target and setting your sights on it, is one of the first steps when you are going to shoot a bow and arrow. It is also the first step in creating a Bullseye Marriage. Unless you have a clear vision of what you are shooting for then you will be hard pressed to even know where to aim. The idea is to develop *a clear concise mental picture* (CCMP) of a great marriage and then strive for that. It will be important to stay in touch with one another and communicate as you move through the various events and stages of life. Those events and stages will most likely add different dimensions and nuances to the clear concise mental picture of what you are targeting together.

Napoleon Hill in his book *Think and Grow Rich* wrote
about individuals who had
achieved riches in their lifetime.
Hill defined riches as anything
you want it to be. He specifically
targeted those who had achieved
financial wealth because it is easy
to measure. He discovered that
there were some similarities in all
the individuals he studied. We
have found that many of the

> *Every person who wins in an undertaking must be willing to cut all sources of retreat. Only by doing so can one be sure of maintaining that state of mind known as a burning desire to win — essential to success.*
>
> Napoleon Hill

steps he revealed to achieve riches could be applied as well to
having a rich marriage. For instance, Hill states that the starting
point for all achievement is desire. The question then, when it
comes to your marriage, is do you have a desire to have a great
relationship with your spouse? If you have been married a while
and are struggling in your relationship you may answer, "I want
a great relationship — I just don't know if it's possible with this
spouse." Maybe you have worked on your relationship in the
past and you do not see that it has moved to what you define as
a great relationship. Our hope and prayer is that as you move
through the exercises in this book, and discuss the various ideas
we put forth that it will assist you, as a couple, in redefining
what you mean when you say "I want a great relationship in
marriage."

Dr. Robert Fontana, Francis' brother, makes the statement, "Marriage works if you work at it." Working on your marriage could mean that you access some of the links that we cite in Chapter 9 to assist you in working towards your Bullseye. Many of the websites and retreats listed have great track records of assisting couples in moving their marriages from bad to good and from good to great. It is worth it to work on your marriage. As the character Katie stated in her monologue at the end of the movie *The Story of Us*, "…it's hard, it's much harder than I thought it would be, but there's more good than bad. And you don't just give up…"

In another great movie, *Apollo XIII*, there is a very tense scene right after the ship has had a series of explosions. Everyone is reporting to Gene Krantz, the flight director, "This is what is wrong with the ship…and this is what is wrong with the ship…and this is what is wrong with the ship…." Finally, Gene Krantz raises his hand and says, "Hold on, we can't get the ship home with what is wrong with the ship, tell me what is right." There is silence as everyone looks at him with a blank face and then responds, "We'll have to get back with you on that." All the engineers turn their focus to what is right with the spacecraft instead of what is wrong with it. In making that slight change in attitude and focus, they are able to see what is working and incredibly get the ship safely home.

FRANCIS: My parents married and had nine pregnancies in the first ten years of their marriage resulting in 7 sons. They had very little time to truly get to know one another as a couple before the responsibilities of raising a family were demanded. Twenty years into their marriage, they realized they were married yet living together as strangers. They found only three things they could agree on:

> *They were married.*

> *They had seven boys.*

> *Divorce was not an option.*

For the next few years life as a married couple was very difficult and challenging. Yet their focus on what was right with their marriage began as a building block to a great relationship. After a few years of intense struggle, the last 15 years of their marriage were their best years before my Dad died at age 61. Just as in the story of Apollo XIII, they learned to focus on what was working and good about their relationship and guided "their ship" home as a witness to all who knew of what a holy, and sacramental marriage is supposed to be.

Our tendency as humans is to focus on what is wrong. We focus on what is wrong with our marriages, our children, and ourselves. Consequently, our tendency is to make our circumstances worse because we are focusing on what is wrong instead of what is right. In sports the best coaches are the ones who watch for strengths in players and utilize those strengths while working on skills that will assist the weak points. It's not being blind to what is wrong, just shifting the focus as Gene Krantz made the engineers do in the movie. In your marriage, begin to recognize and name more of the good than the bad and use those strengths as you work toward developing your Bullseye Marriage target.

Napoleon Hill coined the phrase, "What you can see and believe you can achieve." So focus on seeing yourself in a great relationship with your spouse. What does it look like? What is happening? Use the ideas and thoughts from the Sensory Brainstorm exercise to begin to capture on paper those phrases and ideas that define what a great relationship looks like for you. Maybe there are some key scripture passages or a song or a quote that can be used to assist you in defining your target.

One of the scriptures that we have used through the years to define our target is Luke 10: 25-28. In this passage a lawyer poses a question to Jesus, "What must I do to inherit everlasting life?" Jesus answered him, "What is written in the law? How do you read it?" The lawyer replied, "You shall love the Lord your God with all your heart, with all your soul, with all your strength and with all your mind; and your neighbor as yourself." Jesus said, "You have answered correctly. Do this and you shall live."

> *The eternal perspective should govern the temporal perspective.*

Jesus is answering a question concerning eternal life. Eternal life with God is the ultimate end to keep in mind in our everyday life. We believe that the eternal perspective should govern the temporal perspective. This thought helps us when everyday life is a bit overwhelming and the temporal things such as money, work, raising kids, etc. seem out of sorts. When sickness sets in, or things just seem too much, it has helped us to take a deep breath, take a step back and put things into an eternal perspective.

When the lawyer answers Jesus' question as to how he reads the law, he gives an answer that we have used as the basis of our own Bullseye Marriage. We believe that our marriage should be a reflection of the love God has for His people. God loves unconditionally and we in turn are to love God with all of our strength, our heart, our soul and our mind. We as a couple are called to mirror that love. We do that through sharing our physical self (our whole strength), our emotional life (our whole heart), our spiritual life (our whole soul), and our intellect (our whole mind) with one another. *(Much of this thought came from Sara's study of Carl Jung, a Swiss psychiatrist, when she attended University of St. Thomas)*

The Bullseye for our marriage incorporates all four of the aspects of the quote from the Gospel of St. Luke:

PHYSICAL-We encourage each other to stay physically fit. We include exercise and healthy eating in our daily disciplines. We enjoy sharing ourselves physically with one another and making love on a regular basis.

EMOTIONAL-We make sure that we say the words, "I love you," daily as well as show that love by our actions. We talk about our feelings and work on effective communication.

We focus on giving affirmations and show appreciation for things that the other person does.

SPIRITUAL-This is a central part of who we are. We share the same faith and much of our life is centered on our church life. We pray together, go to church together, read the Bible together and challenge each other to grow spiritually.

INTELLECTUAL -We love a good discussion. We read and share ideas with one another. Using our minds and awareness to build a business together has been a great challenge in this area.

Even though we don't do these things every day, below are some examples of elements of a Bullseye day for us:

> Praying together in the mornings.

> Exercising.

> Helping our agents and clients put into practice products and services of becoming properly protected, debt free, and financially independent.

> Taking notice of something one or the other has done during the day and affirming that action with some sincere words of praise and thanksgiving.

> Coming home and having a meal with the whole family where we share great conversation.

➤ Being demonstrative and affectionate toward each other.

We realized early on that a great relationship in marriage was not a destination. It was not something that we would arrive at one day and say, "Wow, we're here. We have a great relationship!" We discovered that marriage was more like showing up at an archery range every day, getting the target in sight, picking up the bow and arrow and shooting. There are days when we hit the Bullseye. There are other days when we don't but we at least hit the target. Some days we totally miss the target. Then there are those times when we are too tired to even pick up the bow and arrow and try.

What we discovered is that when we knew what a great relationship looked like for us and believed that it was possible for us to have it then we achieved more Bullseye days! It does not happen every day, but we celebrate when it does! We have to work on it. We have to show up, pick up our bow

> *"What you see and believe you can achieve."*
> *Napoleon Hill*

and arrow, and keep developing the skills and getting better. We have to be aware of the other person as we work together. We have to be willing to move beyond selfishness into a selfless love that for us is modeled after Jesus' word and example in Scripture. It is not easy, but it is worth it and incredibly fulfilling! In fact, there are moments of pure joy!

Our sadness is when we meet people whose marriages end after decades together because the couple stopped working at it. Or it could be that one of the persons began to seek happiness outside of the marriage. They stopped investing time and energy into the relationship. They stopped showing up and developing the skills to keep getting better. The great thing about developing a Bullseye Marriage is that both parties realize that perfection is not the objective. The goal is to show up and get better each day. Work on the skills it takes to reach the Bullseye more often then not. Rest, have fun, keep working at it, and when you have those Bullseye Days acknowledge them and celebrate!

CHAPTER THREE:
What's Your Experience?

Love seems the swiftest, but it is the slowest of all growths. No man or woman really knows what perfect love is until they have been married a quarter of a century.

Mark Twain

In Chapter Two we discussed what's your Bullseye? Most likely you are reading this book because you want to target a great relationship in your marriage. Chapter Two provided you an opportunity to discuss what that looks like for you. You started developing a clear, concise, mental picture of what you are shooting for in your marriage.

If you know what your target is and where you want to go, then what is the next question? Think about calling someone and saying, "I need directions to your house." The first question they are going to ask you is, "Where are you coming from?" When we went to Viking Archery, the store clerk's first question was, "What is your experience?" In essence the clerk was asking us, "Where are you coming from? What's your story?" Your story and all of your experiences, good and bad, are where you are coming from. It's important to realize that your spouse's story, your story and the story that you have lived, for better or for worse, is your starting point for a Bullseye Marriage. The graced moments and the challenging moments are all part of it.

On the Feast of the Holy Family several years ago a young priest, Fr. Chris Kulig, was celebrating mass at our parish. During the homily he got up and with great enthusiasm looked out at the congregation and said, "Yesterday, I started a family!" There was dead silence as the congregation tried to put their brains around what it means for a celibate priest to start a family. He then continued, "I celebrated the marriage of a young couple yesterday!" Everyone laughed. He then went on to talk about the Holy Family as the beginning of the Christian story and how every year, within the liturgy of the Roman Catholic mass, and in Christian churches around the world, the story of the Holy Family is shared at Christmas. The story is told so that it gets passed on to the children and so all can learn from it. Fr. Chris shared the story of how his parents had met and talked about the importance of asking the questions so that you know the story of your family. Fr. Chris challenged the teens to go home and ask their parents the question, "How did our story begin?

Several nights later we had a New Year's Eve party at our home. Many of the parents we're sitting around the kitchen table and one of the teens walked in and said, "So, I need to do my homework assignment from Fr. Chris .What is everyone's story?" We then had the most remarkable experience of everyone sharing their beginning story. As Sara sat and listened and watched she realized this needed to be a family retreat! The *Story of Us Retreat* developed from that discussion and we have offered it a number of times in the Houston area. During the retreat we give families an opportunity to write the beginning of their story. For many of the teens and children who attend the retreat it is the first time they have heard how their family began. In the first session on the retreat we always start with the beginning of the Christian Family. The wonderful story, told in the Bible, is one that we all have as part of our heritage. Sara wrote her own version of that beautiful story:

THE STORY OF THE BEGINNING

OF THE CHRISTIAN FAMILY

A long, long time ago there was a young girl named Mary. Mary was engaged to be married to Joseph. However, Mary became pregnant with someone else's child. When Joseph found out that Mary was pregnant he decided that he would not marry her.

One night Joseph had a dream. In the dream an angel appeared to him and said, "Joseph, son of David, have no fear about taking Mary as your wife. It is by the Holy Spirit that she has conceived this child. She is to have a son and you are to name him Jesus because he will save his people from sins." (Matthew 1:20)

When Joseph awoke he believed his dream. Despite how it looked, and the possible embarrassment that he might endure, he chose to do as the angel of the Lord had directed in his dream and bring Mary into his home as his wife. They exchanged marriage vows and thus began their family and our Christian family.

This foundational story of our faith speaks of courage and strength of character in both Mary and Joseph as well as the strength to say 'yes' to God's will despite how it looks, and what others might say. Joseph and Mary chose to follow dreams and God's voice instead of what could be called "common sense". We, as members of the Christian family, can claim that thread of strength as part of our life's tapestry. It can be woven into our own family story and our own marriage story and thus strengthen our family's foundation.

The story of the beginning of the Christian family is part of your salvation history. Your salvation history is the story of how God has interacted in your life through your life experiences and the choices you have made. God started your story at your conception and your birth. You did not choose your parents, the country you were born in, nor the circumstances of your birth. It is the life you were given to live and God was always there, whether you recognized His presence or not. There is no "God-forsaken" place. God invades all parts of your life.

This recognition of how God invades all aspects of life and that you are on a journey for all of eternity with God is what we call an 'eternal life perspective.' This temporal life is actually embedded within and is just a series of chapters in your eternal story. When you have an eternal life perspective, truth is hidden within suffering and joy. It is in the carving of who you are that truth gets chiseled into your core. Your job is not to resist the chiseling – the cuts in your lives. It is in those times that your character is formed.

The word character comes from carve. When everyone else saw a block of marble, Michelangelo saw the David or the Pieta. He just had to chisel away the extra marble. Your life and your marriage is like that masterpiece of Michelangelo. Everyone else may see a block of marble, but God sees the masterpiece that you are and begins to chisel away, forming you bit by bit into that masterpiece. We encourage you to begin to see the masterpiece that God is working toward achieving in your spouse's life by remembering his or her story as it was told to you through the years.

THE MASTERPIECE TIMELINE ACTIVITY FOR YOU AND YOUR SPOUSE

Take a blank piece of paper and draw out your spouse's timeline. Start with his or her birthday and then draw a line ending with the present moment. On the top of the line add significant dates in your spouse's life that you would label as positive moments…moments that brought joy or happiness or were positive changes. We call the moments when things were going well, "graced moments." Under the line add in the challenging moments. Those moments that were difficult or painful. Put on the timeline where your spouse was born, places he or she moved to, siblings, etc.

What's important is to write out the timeline separate from one another and then come together to share. Follow the simple guidelines. The guidelines are key to having a meaningful encounter as you listen to your spouse's version of your story:

1. Allow for uninterrupted time and a secluded place to complete this exercise.

2. Wife goes first. She shares the timeline she has put together about her husband.

3. Husband listens without interruption.

4. After husband's story has been told by his wife, husband says, "Thank you for knowing my story."

5. After saying, "thank you," the husband then adds to the timeline or shares a deeper part of a story, or rounds out a forgotten part.

6. Husband shares the timeline he has put together about his wife.

7. Wife listens without interruption. (Please honor this part!)

8. After wife's story has been told by her husband, wife says, "Thank you for knowing my story."

9. After saying, "thank you," the wife then adds to the timeline or shares a deeper part of the story, or rounds out a forgotten part.

Graced moments

Birth of Spouse   Today

Challenging Moments

During the Bullseye Marriage Conference we provide time for spouses to complete the above exercise. For many participants this simple exercise is the highlight of the conference. It helps them remember injustices and recall good times. It gives them a time to talk about the ups and downs and time to listen to what still bothers them. After completing the exercise, one person said that it shed light on the forgiveness that needed to still take place. Another person commented that she had not realized how much her husband had listened through the years. We received a thank you note from a couple who had been married over 40 years and attended the conference. They said that the timeline reminded them of some things they used to do together and had stopped. They shared their gratitude for the reminder and committed to begin doing those things again.

The important thing is to share the experience. It reveals the wounds, the scars and all the good things as well. Every person comes into marriage with emotional wounds or scars that happened during experiences in their lifetime. More wounds and scars will most likely take place within the marriage. Reviewing the timeline is not always easy but we have found that our discussion of each other's timeline has often been a source of healing and strengthening of our own relationship.

We found a story in Edward Hays book *St. George and the Dragon and the Quest for the Holy Grail* that reveals how to use the tough times in our lives as a source of strength for ourselves and ultimately, our marriage. The story is about a 20th century man named George, who was not a saint, and a dragon with glowing wounds who prepared him for a sacred search. On page 13, the dragon talks about his wounds, *"These old wounds are the source of my power and my insight. Our greatest and worst enemies are our scars, our wounds and our old injuries. As we journey through life we all have been injured – hurt by parents, brothers or sisters, schoolmates, strangers, lovers, teachers…the possible list of guilty is long. Each wound has the power to talk to us. They speak, however, with crooked voices because of the scars. You must not give in to the voice of your scars, the voice of the times you were trusted and were betrayed, loved and were rejected, did your best and were laughed at. Do not give weight to the scars left because you were slighted or were made to feel less than others. Instead, when those voices call to you to react with envious or jealous feelings, do exactly the opposite. When they say run away you must stay. When they whisper, distance yourself, then come all the closer. You must transform their power, not destroy it. That, my friend, is really being involved in a quest. All quests begin with some question. 'How do I find happiness?' That's what you are questing for, George— happiness. And happiness, health, holiness and all the rest come only when we have made our injuries into glorious wounds."*

Times of injury, whether they are physical or mental, are often the times when our character is formed. Injuries normally happen because of our choices. How a couple chooses to heal injuries incurred by their actions will either create a glorious wound that will glow as a time that strengthens their marriage or will be a scar that drives them apart.

In Chapter 6 we go further into what happens when you get tired or hurt. What's important in this chapter is to recognize that the challenging moments and the times of injury in your life need to be named, acknowledged and discussed so you can move forward to make them 'glorious wounds' that have the ability to strengthen your marriage. No one wants to relive the moments that are not good times, but to not discuss them or not bring them out in the open keeps the wound festering instead of healing. You will experience times which are hurtful. It is your choice whether you let those times keep festering or work on healing them and make them glorious wounds. As Scott Peck says in *A World Waiting to Be Born,* "A healthy organization—whether a marriage, a family, or a business corporation—is not one with an absence of problems, but one that is actively and effectively addressing or healing its problems."

It's important to realize that the way you handle problems and the image that you have of a great relationship and a Bullseye Marriage stems from your history and your background. Francis's paternal grandparents were Catholic born in Sicily and came to the United States after an arranged marriage. Like most immigrants, they moved to this county seeking a better opportunity for their family around the turn of the 20th century. His maternal grandparents were Catholic Cajuns. Sara's paternal grandparents were Catholic Cajuns and her maternal grandparents were Methodist and descended from a variety of nationalities including Native Americans. Our cultural and religious makeup is directly correlated to our thoughts on marriage. If we had been born in India and were Muslim we would, of course, be writing a different book on marriage! Our background is Catholic Christian; our culture is Italian, Cajun and mainly Texan and Louisianan. Therefore this is a book about Christian marriage from that perspective.

Christian marriage, itself has a long history and timeline. That history most likely is directly correlated to your understanding of marriage along with your own ancestral background. In looking at a Bullseye Marriage it is important to recognize where your ideas come from and the part they play in your concept of what makes a great relationship. The history of Christian marriage could be a book in itself. As mentioned in Chapter 2, we decided to offer it to our readers in a couple of nutshells found in Chapter 9, the Resource section at the end of the book. Much of the research came from browsing the Internet but our main source was *Doors to the Sacred* by Joseph Martos. We found that so many of the traditions at weddings come down to us through the centuries. More importantly, the basis of what makes up a great marriage can be found at the very beginning of Christianity and throughout history.

What the nutshells revealed to us is that the basis of Christian marriage ultimately goes back to Jesus' words: "Have you not heard that at the beginning the Creator made them male and female and declared that 'for this reason a man shall leave his father and mother and cling to his wife, and the two shall become as one'?" Through the centuries people have attempted to understand just what it means to be transformed from two into one. It certainly is not an easy task.

At our wedding, we asked the priest who witnessed our wedding vows to choose the Gospel reading for us. Fr. Fred Reynolds had walked with us throughout our dating and engagement time. He knew us well. He chose the Palm Sunday Gospel to read at our wedding. As he explained in his homily, *"That is a strange Gospel to read at a wedding, but not at a Christian wedding. In the final days before the crucifixion, everyone told Jesus not to go to Jerusalem because it was too dangerous. Yet, Jesus knew he had to go to Jerusalem. Jesus' ride into Jerusalem was very much like the wedding day – a celebration. And then Jesus went through His Stations of the Cross and ultimately died and then resurrected. You will have your own Stations of the Cross sometime in your life as a couple. You will also have many moments of dying and then resurrecting as you continue to become the couple God is calling you to be. This is part of the process of living the Sacrament of Marriage."*

Christ is there throughout the whole timeline and in every moment of the painful times as well as the good times. Your unique timeline is your unique salvation history. It is your experience. It is the make-up of who you are and who you are becoming. In a Bullseye Marriage, couples choose to use their experiences to begin to grow and become better at having a great relationship. They choose to make their wounds *glorious wounds.* And they recognize the uniqueness of each individual and themselves as a couple.

SARA: My mom and dad met in their high school biology class. Dad walked mom to her next class. After their first date he walked her home. When they graduated from college they walked into the Sacrament of Marriage. My siblings and I were eyewitnesses to Mom and Dad's various marital and family "stations of the cross" as well as the "resurrection" moments. Fifty-five years after they walked down the church aisle together at their wedding, Dad walked with Mom through an illness that eventually took her life. Dad was holding her hand when she died.

Much of the "Stations of the Cross" moments in my parents' marriage came because Mom had a difficult time internally feeling loved by Dad. In many ways that is because she had grown up with a father who never spoke the words, "I love you," until he was on his deathbed. Dad struggled with loving Mom the way she needed to be loved. In the last year of Mom's life, Dad got it right. He retired and spent that last year being attentive to her, anticipating her needs and caring for her the way she really wanted to be cared for in her illness.

About six weeks before Mom died, my siblings and I gathered at my parents' farm to discuss how we would assist in her care. We had a wonderful weekend sharing, talking, making plans and celebrating Mom. On Sunday, Dad went to mass and brought back the Eucharist for Mom. We had a special prayer service, which Dad led, in order for Mom to receive Communion. During the prayer service, Dad read a letter that my mom's sister had sent. It was a beautiful letter of how my aunt had memories of my mom in every part of her home. As Dad read the letter, he broke down and started crying. He couldn't finish the letter. My mom, who had been listening intently to him reading reached out a hand to Dad and I saw for the first time in my life a steady recognition in her eyes that she knew without a doubt that Dad did love her. His sacrificial love gave her that assurance at the end of her life. I was so grateful to be a witness to that "resurrection" moment.

CHAPTER FOUR:
Are you right-handed or left-handed?

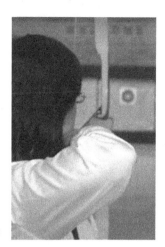

Knowing yourself is the beginning of all wisdom.

Aristotle

Before Sara could even pick up a bow and arrow she had to know whether she was right-handed or left-handed as well as whether she was right-eye dominant or left-eye dominant. Think about sports in general for a minute. Basic knowledge of yourself pervades almost every sport you may choose to play, whether it is baseball, soccer, golf, tennis, football or any other major sport. The more you know about yourself affects your ability to execute the skills of the game as well as your basic enjoyment of it. If Sara had picked up a left-handed bow when she went to the archery range she would have been less successful and it would have been a very frustrating process. Instead, she had knowledgeable individuals asking her questions and assisting her with answering a few basic important questions even before she picked up a bow. In fact, it took two people providing different ideas to assist Sara in learning that she was right-eye dominant and right-handed.

If you apply this same principal found in sports to targeting a great relationship in your marriage then being in touch with yourself and knowing yourself well affects your ability to execute relationship skills as well as your basic enjoyment of marriage. Taking the sports metaphor a step further—if you continuously work on your skills in a sport then your improved abilities most likely will affect any team you play on. You cannot change the other team members' skills but you can influence the team by your improvement and your attitude. The same is true in a relationship; the only person you can change is yourself. However, if you work on becoming the best person you can be by improving your attitude, communication skills, your relationship skills and getting to know yourself better, that influences and affects not only your marriage but also your family and friends.

This is easier said than done. It helps to have others assist in this matter and get advice and ideas from different books and sources. In the Resource Chapter at the end of this book there is a list of books and websites to assist. It's important to remember as you read through books and take personality tests online and learn more about yourself that no person is stagnant; your life experiences and knowledge, shapes your philosophy and outlook. To know yourself is a lifetime process.

The other important thing to remember is you are not an island. To know yourself completely is to acknowledge the people who have formed you through the years and the ones you are directly connected to in the present. Knowing yourself and self-realization does not bring about happiness or satisfaction in a marriage. Marriage is a team "sport." Therefore, in marriage, it is important to not only continuously grow in knowledge of yourself, but also work toward understanding your spouse and encouraging that person to grow.

SARA: Francis and I began our discovery of self even before we got married. My parents were always reading books about relationships and effective communication. One of the books was the Myers-Briggs Temperament Sorter. Myers and Briggs were actually a mother daughter team who took Carl Jung's understanding of personality and developed a set of questions and an answer code that assisted individuals in "discovering" their personality type. Francis and I took the Myers Briggs temperament sorter and, through the years, have continued to grow in our understanding of our personality type. We've also used the Keirsey Temperament Sorter, developed by David Keirsey, which is a shorter version of the Myers-Briggs.

One of the important things we "discovered" was that Francis is an introvert and Sara is an extrovert. What that means is that Sara processes everything outwardly through talking. She needs to have someone to listen to her "think" through an idea before she acts on it. As an extrovert, she is energized by being around people. Francis, on the other hand, processes everything inwardly. He "thinks" through an idea internally and then, when asked, will share it with others. As an introvert, he is energized by being by himself.

The self-knowledge, which the Temperament Sorter gave us, helped us to live in harmony with one another and be more effective in achieving Bullseye days. Sara continues to work on not just blurting out her ideas but letting Francis know that she needs time with him to share ideas. She continues to work on giving Francis his space and time to himself and not just jumping in with her words. Francis continues to work on sharing the ideas in his head and being present and listening to Sara. He encourages Sara in getting together with friends and is always open to small social gatherings. Another important thing Francis has learned is that after large gatherings he needs to take time to "re-energize" himself through quiet time alone.

The Temperament Sorter and the various personality tests we have taken through the years continue to help us understand ourselves and the best way to work together in our marriage. In our Primerica business we use a system developed by Jim Hoyt, which he calls the STAR system. STAR stands for *Stability, Theory, Action, and Relationship*. Jim teaches this wonderful system exclusively to Primerica agents, but we have found it is effective not only in developing our business but in our relationship. We have learned for instance, that Francis is an Action oriented person. Sara is a Stability person. Francis is always ready for action and change. Sara does not like change and prefers watching people in action.

SARA: A great example of this happened on a trip to Hawaii. Our hotel room had an incredible view of Diamondback Mountain and the lagoon below us. I was ready to get a good book and go and sit by the pool or even on the beach. Francis, however, observed from our balcony that people were surfing in the lagoon. He was ready to go and wanted me to go with him! I somewhat reluctantly gave up my vision of lying sedately by the pool, which I could do anywhere, and away we went. We had a blast! We hired a surfing instructor and I actually was able to ride a small wave—more like a water bump—all the way onto the beach. I have to say that marriage to Francis continues to be an adventure. He calls me out of my routine and into the fun of life.

FRANCIS: Sara, on the other hand, challenges me to get in touch with my inner emotions when often it is easier to not "go there." My tendency is to not say anything about my emotions but to just listen to Sara's monologue. I have learned over the years that it is not enough just to listen. Sara desires reciprocal feedback. For us to have a deeper relationship, I must engage my senses and thoughts into whatever it is she is wrestling with and enter into a dialogue with her. She challenges me to keep growing and becoming more in touch with whom I am as a person and who God is calling me to become.

The various books, programs and websites that we have used through the years have helped us improve our knowledge of ourselves, our communication skills and definitely increased our ability to have Bullseye days in our marriage. You may have other programs at your work that you have used, or other books or websites. In a Bullseye Marriage the important element is to become the best person you can be through self-knowledge and share the discovery with your spouse.

Part of that discovery of yourself is acknowledgement of those things you had no control over as your character was formed: who your parents were, where you were born, what country you were born in, your siblings and most of your early life. Those elements in your life formed much of what you like or dislike, many of your opinions, your life skills and how you approach life and even marriage. Acknowledgement of those aspects in your life assists in getting to know yourself better and then working toward becoming a better person.

SARA: I was the youngest child for ten years. By the time I was twelve I had become the middle child because my two younger brothers were born. When I was fifteen, I became the oldest at home because both of my sisters had moved out of the house. So I mainly have youngest child tendencies but have been the youngest, the middle and the oldest. I have lived on both coasts of the United States (California, Maryland, and North Carolina) and in the middle of the United States (Kansas, Texas and Louisiana). I have attended private school, Catholic school and public school. I always laugh and tell everyone that I am balanced because of my early years! My mother was raised Protestant and converted to Catholicism when she married my dad. My dad was Catholic all his life. He read every Encyclical (Papal letter) that was written and my mother questioned every Encyclical that was written. We had lively discussions at the dinner table as well as arguments on beliefs and faith. I grew up having family meetings and assigned chores and parents who read the Bible, books on the Catholic faith and lots of psychology books. My tendency today is to gather information from multiple sources, try to understand all sides of an issue, talk about issues and discuss effective ways of dealing with things and look for what can be learned from any given situation. I do not like to do things unless I can see the purpose in them. The core value that I was taught was we should make a positive difference in the world and that our faith in God was a key element in making that difference. Consequently, my Catholic faith has been a central part of my life and directly influenced all key decisions.

FRANCIS: I was the fifth of seven boys born and raised in Abbeville, Louisiana (the heart of Cajun Country). I attended a small Catholic school all the way through high school. Growing up in a family of seven boys created a strong testosterone environment. We lived on the edge of town across the street from the Catholic schools we were attending. On the other side of the street were the rice fields and irrigation canals for farming; these became our playgrounds for adventures and exploration. Growing up in Deep South Louisiana, we were living in a sportsman's paradise and were able to learn to hunt and fish at an early age.

Both of my parents were music educators. My dad was the high school band director at Abbeville High School (the public school). Mom taught private piano lessons in our home and accompanied the elementary and high school choirs at Mount Carmel Elementary and Vermilion Catholic High School. Because of a small enrollment in the high school (I graduated with fifty classmates), both the athletic department and the music department had to cooperate with each other for the pool of students. Consequently, I could participate in all aspects of student activities.

Academic, sports, and music participation at the Catholic school fostered the core family values my parents wanted to pass on. Some of these, in no particular order were Competition, Sportsmanship, Teamwork, Work Ethic, Leadership, Honesty, Integrity, Strong Moral Character and love of God. Mom and Dad were intentional about wanting to pass on to their sons the "light of faith" of the Roman Catholic Church. They trusted the Catholic school system to be their partner and, for the most part, it worked.

The dark cloud in our family was family secrets. Apparently, manic depression is a family trait which came from my maternal grandfather's side of the family, yet somehow this was not discussed. To give credit to my parents and their generation, however, little was known about the disease at that time. My mother's psychological health became an issue early on in our lives growing up. I was totally unaware of the mental illness of mom but she would disappear for weeks on end and all I knew was she was sick and in a hospital. We never went to visit her nor do I recall ever talking about the illness of manic depression or bi-polar as it is referred to today.

During my teenage years I remember the first time this came to light. We had a family meeting, with our parish priest in attendance, and

mom revealed to all of us where she had been going and that she had a
mental illness called manic depression. I was stunned! Shocked! Was mom
crazy? I did not know what this meant but it did not sound like the
mother I knew. We were not encouraged to ask questions about this or
other aspects of life and so I accepted this new information as a fact of life
about mom.

About this same time a miracle happened. Mom and Dad
rediscovered their faith through the Catholic Charismatic Renewal. Their
faith life took on an entirely new dimension. Religion and faith became
very personal to my parents. There were some key benefits of this renewal of
faith:

> *They got more involved in their journey of faith with the church*
> *parish and the community of believers.*

> *New people came into their inner circle of life who was also in this*
> *rediscovery of their faith life.*

> *There was a new spark in their marriage as they began to*
> *rediscover each other throughout the process of rediscovering the*
> *faith.*

> *As a teenager, I witnessed a change in their attitudes about life*
> *and their belief in the gospel values of Jesus Christ. They actually*
> *believed all this "stuff" being taught in our religion classes at the*
> *Catholic School.*

> *Because of my witnessing their belief, prayers, and positive*
> *experiences, I accepted the renewal as a fact of life.*

In summary, I learned that walking in faith with your marriage partner was a very valuable thing. To learn to pray together as a couple and read the scriptures daily were some fundamental changes that helped my parents start hitting the Bullseye in their marriage.

Because of how we were raised, the teachings and doctrines of the Catholic Church and principles found in the Bible formed us as people and consequently were key elements from the very beginning of our relationship. They are central to our definition of what a Bullseye Marriage looks like for us and what we target on a daily basis.

At the core of our marriage is the greatest commandment, "love God with your whole mind, your whole heart, your whole soul, with all your strength and love your neighbor as yourself." That commandment cries out for us to know ourselves. We have to love ourselves in order to fully love our neighbor and we have to know our own mind, our own heart, our own soul and our own physical body in order to fully open ourselves to love God fully.

In marriage, the closest neighbor is our spouse. So we are called to love our spouse as we love our self. This is not an easy task if we are struggling to love our self or do not even know our self that well. Think about it— usually when you have had a bad day at work, or something has happened in your life and you not feeling that great about yourself, those are the times it is most difficult to show love to your spouse. Most marriages become rocky if they rely fully on the spouses just loving each other the way they personally love themselves. The

Catholic Catechism teaches, *"The Sacrament of Matrimony signifies the union of Christ and the Church. It gives spouses the grace to love each other with the love with which Christ has loved his Church; the grace of the sacrament thus perfects the human love of the spouses, strengthens their indissoluble unity, and sanctifies them on the way to eternal life."* (Catholic Catechism 1661)

In a Christian marriage then, spouses are called to go beyond self-love and indulgence to a love for the other through service, gentle affection, and generosity of spirit, active deeds and mutual help. Marriage is a process of growing and deepening in love, nurtured by the Spirit of Christ. This is possible when we identify with the original purpose of marriage. In the Gospels Jesus explained, "Have you not heard that at the beginning the Creator made them male and female and declared that 'for this reason a man shall leave his father and mother and cling to his wife, and the two shall become as one'? Thus, they are no longer two but one flesh. Therefore, let no man separate what God has joined." (Matthew 19:3-12, Mark 10:2-12, Luke 16:18). Jesus declares the scriptural doctrine he quotes from Genesis to be God's ultimate intent for marriage in human society.

The deepest and fullest unity in our marriage comes when we acknowledge God's love for the other and work toward loving that person as God loves them. It is a sacrificial love that somehow is fullest, more life-giving and happiest when working towards the good of the other.

Sara's mother, Joy Guidroz, called that the Platinum Rule. The Golden Rule is, "Do unto others the way you want them to do unto you." (Matthew 7:12, Luke 6:31) The Platinum Rule in marriage is, "Do for your spouse the way they want to be done to." The basic premise is that we have a tendency to try to

love our spouse the way we want to be loved instead of learning their "love language," as Gary Chapman refers to it in his book *The Five Love Languages.* When spouses follow the Platinum Rule and communicate the way they want to be loved with each other, more Bullseyes can be hit. The key in all of this is knowing yourself and what your love language is and taking the responsibility to communicate it to your spouse. You then must go the next step and take responsibility for learning your spouse's needs and love them the way they want to be loved; in essence, becoming a "student" of the other person. To achieve this rule requires communication, knowing what the other wants and choosing into words and actions that lift their spirits and working toward the other person's happiness.

The best story to explain the Platinum Rule is a rather silly story about a married couple and chicken. Whenever she cooked chicken, the wife always made sure to give her husband the breast meat because that was her favorite part. She loved her husband so much she wanted to give him what she enjoyed best. She took for herself her least favorite parts of the chicken, the legs and thighs. This went on for 25 years of marriage until one day the husband finally asked, "Wife, why do you always take the best part of the chicken for yourself and give me the part I like least?" The wife started to cry, "I did not know that you liked the legs and thighs. I was giving you the part I liked best because I thought that is what you liked as well." For 25 years they had not communicated what each really wanted. They were following the Golden Rule and doing for the other, as they would want to be done to—the wife giving the chicken she liked and the husband taking it without any question. The good news is once this couple communicates and follows the Platinum Rule they both will get the part of chicken they have wanted for 25 years!

True sacrificial love does not necessarily mean that you give up what you want. It means knowing what you want and need, communicating that with your spouse, then listening, learning and acting on what your spouse wants and needs.

SARA: My mom and dad are prime examples of working on the Platinum Rule. Mom loved to be cared for, given gifts and praise and have people notice and positively comment on things she did. She needed to be touched and hugged. Dad, on the other hand, needed very little recognition. He did not need to be told how great something was that he accomplished. He needed less touch than my mother. Mom always had a desire for Dad to be more present in the way she wanted and needed him to be. When Dad retired they went to a therapist for 5 sessions in order to get in sync with one another. Much of what they worked on was communication. I had a great talk with my dad soon after the therapy sessions had ended. Dad said that one of the reasons he retired was so that he could be more present to Mom in the next years of their marriage. Mom had had some health challenges and Dad set aside himself in order to be present to her and love her the way she wanted to be loved. The key to hitting the Bullseye is to do this willingly and communicate well. When both people are doing this you definitely have a Bullseye Marriage!

As Aristotle states, "Knowing yourself is the beginning of all wisdom." Sharing that wisdom with your spouse and respectfully accepting the self that your partner shares with you, lays the foundation for a Bullseye Marriage.

CHAPTER FIVE:
Men & Women
Shoot Differently

I got married with the idea that I would shape Tony into the husband I wanted him to be. Somehow it didn't work out that way. Tony didn't cooperate.

Evelyn Trahan Fontana, Francis' mother

In archery, a bow is strung differently for a man than it is for a woman because men and women shoot differently. It is based on their strength. The differences between men and women are apparent not only in sports but also described in the Book of Genesis in the Bible and even in the latest medical studies which confirm that the brains of men and women are structured differently.

Both men and women have a right and left hemisphere in their brains. Each hemisphere is specialized for different operations. The right hemisphere is used for spatial memory, mathematics and logical thinking. The left hemisphere is used for things related to speech, language, reading and writing. The difference between the genders is the connectors between the two hemispheres. Recent studies reveal that women have a thicker bridge of neural fibers connecting the two hemispheres than men do. As Mark Gungor explains in his *Laugh Your Way to a Better Marriage* seminars, men's brains are compartmentalized into little boxes. When a man is working on something he opens up that compartment in his brain and focuses on that task. Men literally are kings at single-minded focus. Women's brains, on the other hand, are more wired and connected. That is why a woman is better at multi-tasking because she can use more than one brain compartment at a time. As the song goes:

"Well I can rub and scrub till this house shines just like a
dime
Feed the baby
Grease the car
Powder my nose at the same time.

Cause I'm a woman, W-o-m-a-n
Let me tell ya again. I'm a woman
W-o-m-a-n

I'm a Woman" by Jerry Leiber and Mark Stoller

Because of the way a woman's brain is wired she has a difficult time shutting down. Her brain is always active. Men, on the other hand, can literally shut down and think of nothing. Mark Gungor calls that the, "nothing box". So when a woman asks a man, 'what are you thinking?' and he replies 'nothing'; he really is thinking of nothing. Women cannot understand anyone thinking of nothing because they do not have a "nothing box" in their brain.

Of course the above description of the brain is a large generality. Everyone's brain is unique. As Rita Carter states in her book, *Mapping the Mind,* "The human brain is made of many parts. Each has a specific function; to turn sounds into speech; to process color; to register fear; to recognize a face or distinguish a fish from fruit. But this is no static collection of components. Each brain is unique, ever changing and exquisitely sensitive to its environment...Brain activity is controlled by currents and chemicals and mysterious oscillations. The whole is bound together in a dynamic system of systems that does millions of different things in parallel. It is probably so complex that it will never succeed in comprehending itself. Yet it never ceases to try." [1]

Yes, we keep on trying to understand ourselves and the other gender. Countless songs remind us that we just will never comprehend the opposite sex; and yet we not only keep on trying but also work at changing them to become more like us! As Francis' mother stated at our wedding, "I got married with the idea that I would shape Tony into the husband I wanted him to be. Somehow it didn't work out that way. Tony didn't cooperate." The reality is when we try to change another person, we wind up frustrated. In working on and changing ourselves we have the ability to influence and change our environment and those around us. So the key is working on our self and communicating what we learn about ourselves to our spouse.

For our wedding we asked our parents to choose a Scripture reading that was important to them and read that

---

[1] <u>Mapping the Mind</u>, by Rita Carter. University of California Press. 1998. p. 10

Bible passage at our wedding as a gift to us. We knew that Francis's parents would choose the Scripture from 1 Peter 3:1-7: "You married women must obey your husbands, so that any of them who do not believe in the word of the Gospel may be won over apart from preaching, through their wives conduct...You husbands, too, must show consideration for those who share your lives. Treat women with respect as the weaker sex, heirs just as much as you to the gracious gift of life. If you do so nothing will keep your prayers from being answered."

There is a lot of truth in that scripture if you apply it to a few of the differences between men and women. Peter was urging women to use their actions and not nagging or excessive amount of words to make a point. However, husbands need to take notice and show consideration and care for their wives. Even though our strengths are different we all share in the wonderful gift of life. If we acknowledge that mutuality of purpose then we hit the Bullseye!

Of course, there are those who believe, as the mother shared in the movie *My Big Fat Greek Wedding*, "the man is the head of the household, but the woman is the neck and she can turn the man any way she wants to." Men's brains are bigger than women's brains. This size difference has absolutely nothing to do with intelligence, but is explained by the difference in physical size between men and women. Men need more neurons to control their greater muscle mass and body size, thus generally have a larger brain.[2]

The difference in men's and women's brains also creates a whole slew of differences when it comes to our needs. We are all individuals and composed uniquely, however, there is enough consistency in the similarities of the basic needs between sexes to warrant a discussion. Willard F. Harley, Jr. Ph.D. wrote an entire a book on this subject called *His Needs, Her Needs*. He has helped thousands of couples improve their troubled marriages. In his work with couples, Dr. Harley put together a list of 10 emotional needs that were present in both the husband and the wife. Five tend to be rated by women as most important and the other five are rated by men as most important:

THE MAN'S MOST BASIC NEEDS
1. Sexual fulfillment
2. Recreational companionship
3. Physical Attractiveness
4. Domestic Support
5. Admiration

THE WOMAN'S MOST BASIC NEEDS
1. Affection
2. Conversation
3. Honesty and openness
4. Financial support
5. Family commitment[3]

---

[2] http://www.mastersofhealthcare.com/blog/2009/10-big-differences-between-mens-and-womens-brains/ by Amber Hensely

[3] His Needs Her Needs: Building an Affair Proof Marriage. By Willard F. Harley Jr. Fleming H. Revell a division of Baker Book House, 2001, p182-184.

Dr. Harley believes that any husband or wife can make themselves irresistible to their spouse by learning to meet his or her five most important emotional needs. Dr. Harley does a great job in explaining each of the basic needs and ways to utilize knowledge of that need to develop positive habits which move your marriage to a whole different level. On his website, www.marriagebuilders.com he has a list of questionnaires that assist couples in learning about the differences in their emotional needs, things which he calls "love busters"— those things that a person does which have a tendency to annoy or irritate the other.

Dr Harley talks about the importance of making deposits in the Love Bank account. The Love Bank contains different accounts, one for each person you know. Each person either makes deposits or withdrawals whenever we interact with him or her. Pleasurable interactions cause deposits and painful interactions cause withdrawals. As life goes on the accounts in your personal Love Bank fluctuate. [4] If a person causes you more pain than pleasure, then they have taken out more withdrawals from the Love Bank. If there has been more "withdrawals" from the Love Bank than deposits, then that person is in the red with you.

SARA: Francis does an amazing job at making deposits in my Love Bank on a daily basis. He never fails to say, "I love you" every day, he is

---

[4] His Needs, Her Needs: Building an Affair Proof Marriage, by Willard F. Harley Jr.. Fleming H. Revell a division of Baker Book House, 2001. p. 26.

very conscious of taking the time to listen to me and ask about what is on my mind. Our evening ritual of taking a bath together fulfills my need for affection, hugs and cuddling along with conversation. Often times the bath time leads to sexual fulfillment for Francis as well ☺. So bath time ritual fulfills both of our needs. Francis' challenge is in the area of fulfilling my emotional need of "Openness and honesty". As described by Dr. Harley on page 182 of his book, the wife's need for openness and honesty is fulfilled when the husband "describes his positive and negative feelings, events of his past, his daily schedule and his plans for the future." Francis has to work at freely describing his feelings and I normally have to ask him about his daily schedule. He keeps working on fulfilling that need.

FRANCIS: Sara is awesome in making deposits in my "Love Bank" in the areas of Sexual fulfillment, Physical attractiveness and Domestic support. She has gotten better through the years at fulfilling my emotional need of Admiration as described by Dr. Harley as "avoiding criticizing him and reminding him of his value and achievements". The one area she and I have discussed that she fulfills rarely is Recreational companionship. I like to do practically all things outdoors; sculling, kayaking, fishing, hunting, bird watching, gardening, biking, hiking and so forth. For example: I joined a hunting and fishing lease back in the mid 1990s to teach the kids how to hunt and fish. It became a place where the kids and I created some great memories together and occasionally we actually caught fish. Over the twenty years of being a member of the lease, Sara never went to the property. Early in our marriage (before kids) Sara owned a horse and that is an activity she thoroughly enjoys. I would often do that with her. We have been on a number of trail rides with the kids. But I seem to have challenging experiences with horses, like being thrown off of them, so it is not one of my favorite things to do. We do enjoy dancing together but we have not scheduled that on a regular basis and it seems to be limited to attending weddings. We need to keep looking for the recreational activity that we can enjoy together.

(2018 update: I started playing golf on a regular basis and Sara has now started joining me. We've gone to some great golf courses and I think we have finally found something recreational that we both enjoy!)

The list of needs is important to discuss as a couple. We urge you to go to www.marriagebuilders.com to learn more about Dr. Harley's basic concepts and discover your most important needs. Once you know what the other person needs, then you can be more effective in making deposits in their Love Bank each day.

Francis' father, Tony, died of a heart attack while playing golf with a good friend. His friend said that they were at a particular hole that had a large water hazard that Tony never could get his ball over when they played together. On the day Tony died, he hit the ball and it actually went over the water hazard and landed on the fairway. Tony had a heart attack that killed him instantly after taking his second shot from the fairway. Francis' mother revealed her knowledge of Tony's needs list when she shared that story with individuals. She always said that Tony died doing his second favorite thing (recreational companionship) and she is glad that he died in that manner and not doing his first favorite thing (sexual fulfillment).

Shortly after Tony died Evelyn was the guest speaker at a men's prayer breakfast. Tony had started this monthly gathering several years before. Evelyn shared about their marriage with the breakfast club members. She told them it was Tony who kept the romance in their marriage and, in her words; it was the little trimmings that he brought to their marriage that made it successful. Toward the end of their marriage, when they both had stopped trying to get each other to change and started working on themselves, they moved into more fulfillment than she ever thought possible. As she stated, "We prayed together, made love together, enjoyed each other's' company, and time with others." In other words they hit the Bullseye!

Tony and Evelyn Fontana hit the Bullseye because they did not give up on their marriage. Remember, though, at one point in time all they could agree on was that they had seven sons and that divorce was not an option. At that time they began working on themselves and what they wanted in marriage. It was during this time that the scripture they read at our wedding (1 Peter 3:1-7) became central to their marriage.

As Evelyn related at our wedding, she and Tony had received the answer to their prayers by being true to the actions, which that scripture encourages. It wasn't easy; they had to work at their marriage. But it was worth it, because as Evelyn shared at the men's breakfast, she and Tony achieved more happiness than either one of them had ever dreamed possible.

REFLECTION ON SEXUAL FULFILLMENT IN MARRIAGE

It has been 8 years since the first edition of our book. In that short period of time we've seen the rise of smartphones and, consequently, the rise in pornography addiction. Before the internet became so widespread if someone wanted to access pornography they had to purchase magazines, videos or go out to a theater. Pornography was viewed more like alcohol, something not for children to consume but okay for adults in moderation.   We unconsciously adopted that view early in our marriage.

As we became more familiar with St. Pope John Paull II Theology of the Body and the writings of Christopher West our views changed. We began to recognize pornography had no place in a sacramental relationship. "Pure men and women see the mystery of Christ

> *Pornography has no place in a sacramental relationship.*

revealed in their bodies….and feel it in their hearts. They realize that the call to union inscribed in their sexuality is a "great mystery" that proclaims the union of Christ and the Church. When we experience this as the "content" of our sexual attractions, we don't want to lust – we want to genuflect. The "great mystery" of sexuality fills us with profound amazement, awe and wonder. In other words, it fills us with reverence for Christ." (Theology of the Body for Beginners, Christopher West, p. 79)

Instead of "buying into" the secular idea that we should "fulfill each other's sexual fantasies" we have moved into the true freedom of loving God through our affection and sexual fulfillment.

CHAPTER SIX:
What Happens
When You Get Tired?

There is no need for couples to resign themselves to an inevitable downward spiral or a tolerable mediocrity. On the contrary, when marriage is seen as a challenge that involves overcoming obstacles, each crisis becomes an opportunity to let the wine of their relationship age and improve.

Pope Francis, THE JOY OF LOVE

The Great Wall of China is one of the seven man-made wonders of the world. It is a wall that is over 1500 miles long with watchtowers at regular intervals. Archers would stand at a tower location and shoot an arrow  to set the distance between watchtowers. Wherever that arrow landed another archer would stand and shoot another arrow in the opposite direction. That then determined where the next tower would be because soldiers could then stand at the towers and defend the entire wall.

We had the privilege of being able to spend a day hiking a 10-kilometer stretch of the Great Wall. The wall was in disrepair in some sections so we had to tread lightly and carefully. In some places it was so steep it was more like rock

climbing; in others it was smooth and easy to walk. The best part of hiking on The Wall was the towers. The towers represented a time for rest and recuperation. They also marked how far we had come and how far we were going. We would hike a section and then get to the tower and be able to assess our progress. At the towers we could take pictures from the windows looking out at the landscape, eat a snack, sit for a minute and prepare ourselves to make the journey to the next tower. The hike was difficult and treacherous at times, easy at others, fun, exhilarating and exhausting. Walking on the wall was a great adventure.

The whole experience became a metaphor to us for marriage and life. Marriage is a great adventure that is wrought with difficult and treacherous moments, as well as easy moments. Marriage is fun, exhilarating and exhausting. There is a need to stop every now and then for rest and recuperation.

We now call those moments of rest and recuperation "Tower Time." Tower Time could be an individual retreat, a couple's retreat, a week-long vacation, a day or just a moment in the day. Tower Time should be a time to rest and recuperate as well as reflect on how far we have come and where we are going. It is a time to rejuvenate and prepare for the next part of the journey.

One of Sara's favorite Tower Times when the kids were little was an annual "no-demand" retreat that she would schedule during Easter weekend. Francis would set aside time to be home with the kids and she would go to a local retreat house for her own personal retreat. She would bring her Bible, journals, and books that would guide her. The retreat center provided the meals and Sara would sleep, pray, eat, take walks, read and do whatever she wanted – with no demands by anyone but herself. When all four kids were young, that anticipated "no-demand" retreat was much needed. It gave Sara a time to rest and recuperate, delight in having no demands for a few days and be ready for the next part of the journey.

On a journey, all of us get tired. Marriage is a journey and you will get tired. You will need your Tower Time, either as a couple or separately, to rest and rejuvenate for the next part of the journey. Sometimes just the anticipation that Tower Time is coming helps you get through the steps of the journey. When you hit rough spots along the way as a couple, it's important to communicate and know when Tower Time is needed.

Sometimes outside help is needed to assist you after a particularly hard part of the journey.

For example, when Francis' mom died, Francis went to see a friend who is a Christian therapist in order to assist him through his grief. Grief is a tiring part of the journey of life. It makes you want to stop aspects of life and pay attention to it. All of us will experience the loss of someone close. During that time it's important to take the time to stop a moment and pay attention to the grief process. Give it some Tower Time before you continue on your journey. If you don't take Tower Time after you've lost a loved one then your body will force you to stop. Your grief will manifest itself in some form of illness or ache in your own body. Sara experienced that after a very good friend died several years ago.

SARA: I had had the experience of family members dying, but never a close friend. Patty and Rick had been our best friends. We were in each other's weddings and had been at the hospital right after the births of each of our children. We prayed together, laughed together and cried together. Patty died of Leukemia and we walked with her, Rick and their three children as she fought to stay alive. I thought that I had grieved and processed her death, but the reality is I like to be in control and did not want to start crying for fear of never being able to stop. I kept pushing down the tears of sadness until eventually the grief manifested itself in physical symptoms. I sought Chiropractors, and Doctors until finally a co-worker and friend, who was also good friends with Patty, gently confronted me with the question, "Sara, when are you going to allow yourself to grieve for Patty?" At that moment, I began to cry uncontrollably. I told her, "this is why I

Memories of Patty

A wounded healer, reaching out because of her hurt; strengthened by her pain, she gave freely.

A gentle kind spirit, strong in character.

Devoted daughter, caring sister, good friend, who loved James Coney Island Hot Dogs and quiet conversations.

Her flute sounded merrily, playfully, longingly and gently – calling forth joy in the Lord.

Loving wife, example of motherhood, calmly listening to her children's stories, enjoying time with them, juggling schedules, connecting, praying, working, walking with her husband and her children towards eternal life.

May she rest in the arms of the Lord and may the music of her flute and the memory of her life forever resound in our hearts.

---

didn't want to start crying; I don't know when it will end!" The uncontrollable tears did stop eventually. It took letting go and allowing the tears to flow for my physical symptoms to also begin to be relieved. That evening I took a long walk and recognized my great sadness. As I spoke with Francis, I began to realize that through all of Patty's treatments and throughout her illness I had done everything to avoid the grieving process or recognition that she was going to die. I would do things that needed to be done, like watch the kids, in order to avoid going up and seeing her in the hospital. Francis had walked with her and grieved along the way; my grief snuck up on me because I kept pushing it away. Once I recognized that I had really not grieved; I took some time to process and walk through the grief. I wrote poems, because that is the way I process things, prayed and cried.

Tower Time is not just for after the treacherous or difficult times. Tower time is as simple as daily prayer or even an evening of games and laughter with good friends or the whole family. Just as the Great Wall was built with watchtowers placed intentionally far enough apart to fend off enemies, intentionally planning Tower Time in your marriage and in your life helps fend off the "enemies of your marriage." Remember that Tower Time should be planned for you as an individual as well as a couple. Communication is key here as you construct how far the towers will be. Sara actually takes a Tower Time every morning when she rises before everyone else and spends time in prayer. We plan Tower Times as a couple by scheduling date nights or time with the family.

FRANCIS: I take a Tower Time by getting to the office before anyone else and spending time praying the Liturgy of the Hours. I also go sculling in Clear Lake or Galveston Bay. Spending time alone in God's creation whether golfing, hiking, fishing, sculling, kayaking, hunting, or just walking my dog is a great Tower Time for me.

So what happens when you get tired or hurt? Take some Tower Time, seek help, and communicate your needs to your spouse. Maybe there is a need to attend a couples retreat or couples' counseling in order to get back on target. In Chapter 9 there is a list of retreats that may be exactly what you need for Tower Time. They will provide you a place to learn new skills; give you time to focus on what you are targeting together and assist in any healing and forgiveness that may need to take place. A counselor who believes in marriage should be able to help you in developing effective communication skills as well as assist in mediating issues that need to be resolved. Please note that there are therapists and counselors out there who are not effective marriage counselors. Take the time to interview several counselors prior to choosing one that will work for you as a couple.

There are many temptations and trials that will come "like a thief in the night to steal and kill and destroy" your marriage. We stand on Jesus' promise in John 10:10 that He came so that we "might have life and have it to the full." As a husband and wife we must stand firm together and seek the fullness of life. Maybe because of events or circumstances it is time to talk about what the Bullseye looks like and rework what you are targeting. When the time is right and you are rejuvenated and rested pick up your bow and start shooting. A Bullseye is waiting for you once again. It is worth it to pick up the bow and shoot for the fullness of life in your marriage.

CHAPTER SEVEN:
Tips for Hitting
the Bullseye

"To keep your marriage brimming, with love in the loving cup,
whenever you're wrong admit it; whenever you're right shut up."

Ogden Nash

Proudly displayed on the wall at Viking Archery
are targets of archers who achieved all bullseyes at a
particular practice or event. When Sara asked how often a
perfect set of bullseyes happens, she was told, "very rarely
…but the archers who choose to show up on a regular
basis and practice the most are the ones who achieve the
best scores." A successful marriage that hits the bullseye
more often than not happens because spouses choose to
"show up" on a regular basis and work on their marriage.
A couple who desires a Bullseye marriage chooses the
daily disciplines that will assist in targeting a sacramental
relationship. Couples recognize that they have to be aware
of each other and practice some basic skills. This chapter
shares some quick tips to assist in your daily Bullseye
target practice. The tips come from the Bullseye Marriage
Seminars, our own ideas, as well as actions we witnessed

from other couples. You will most likely have other ideas to add to the list. Share them with others; we all need effective tips for hitting the bullseye!

- ➢ Thank your spouse for even the things that are expected. Someone cooks dinner, takes the trash out, puts away the dishes, mows the lawn… all the things that need to be done in the house…acknowledge the person by saying, "Thank you."

- ➢ Don't allow "put downs" to invade your home. Work on building up one another through your words and your actions.

- ➢ Do not participate in wife or husband bashing. Speak well of your spouse to others. Focus on the positives and speak that to others. Build your spouse up in front of them and when you are away from them.

- ➢ Remember that the only person you have control over is yourself. You can influence your spouse with your positive words, actions and attitude…that is all. Nagging and attempting to force someone to do something normally drives him or her to do the opposite of what you want them to do.

- ➢ Take the time to make a list of 100 things you love about your spouse. Share those 100 things by writing one a day for 100 days on sticky notes and leaving it on the bathroom mirror for him or her to read.

- ➢ If you are finding yourself focusing on the negative, do an attitude adjustment by looking for the positive in a situation or what you could be doing differently to positively change the circumstances.

- ➢ Be aware that when you are frustrated by something your spouse is doing or not doing it could be directly correlated to something that you are doing or not doing. Look to yourself and your actions first.

- ➢ Work on communicating effectively. Take classes in communication and read books. Talk respectfully with one another.

- ➢ Go on date nights.
- ➢ Keep God first, your spouse second and your children third.
- ➢ Be willing to forgive and ask for forgiveness.
- ➢ "...Anticipate each other in showing respect." (Romans 12:10) Be respectful in your words and actions even when you argue.
- ➢ Go on marriage retreats and seminars together.
- ➢ Volunteer at Church together.
- ➢ Have game nights with other couples and families; keep a sense of humor and laughter.
- ➢ Keep the romance alive – light some candles, put on good music and dance together. Or take an evening stroll together.
- ➢ Have a date night starting at the computer and taking the Love Language Assessment located at www.garychapman.com. Then go out to eat and discuss what you discovered about the way you need to be loved. Share with your spouse the best way for him/her to show you love.
- ➢ Once you know your spouse's love language, be intentional about doing one thing daily to love your spouse the way they need to be loved.
- ➢ Give your spouse coupons to redeem for fun things or things you know they would like. For example, "coupon good for an hour long massage" or "coupon good for a movie night" or "coupon good for dinner with friends." Be creative.
- ➢ Instead of saying "I'm sorry" and expecting your spouse to say, "it's okay," ask for forgiveness by using the words, "Will you forgive me for......?" Then allow your spouse to respond to your question. Allow this to be a dialogue of reconciliation and move you both to a place of asking and receiving forgiveness.

➢ Remember your wedding day. Remember the vows you spoke to one another. Say them to each other again on your anniversary or even once a month. Below is one example:

The bridegroom *says: I, (Name), take you, (Name), to be my wife. I promise to be true to you in good times and in bad, in sickness and in health. I will love you and honor you all the days of my life.*

The bride *says: I, (Name), take you, (Name), to be my husband. I promise to be true to you in good times and in bad, in sickness and in health. I will love you and honor you all the days of my life.*

If you were married in the Catholic Church the vows are a key part of the moment you were ministers of the Sacrament of Marriage. As ministers remember the importance of the daily discipline of prayer individually and with one another. We have incorporated a variety of ways of prayer into our daily and weekly routine:

➢ Participating in Mass together

➢ Listening to the Daily Scripture readings while we do our morning stretches. (we use the Laudate app for the readings and to read the lives of the Saints.)

➢ Francis prays the evening Liturgy of the Hours aloud each night when we've crawled into bed…usually Sara falls asleep as he reads them ☺

➢ Saying a Rosary together .

➢ Going for a walk and saying the Divine Mercy Chaplet.

➢ Praying grace before meals

➢ Praying in the car as we begin a road trip.

➢ Spending time in Eucharistic Adoration

➢ Reading the Bible together.

CHAPTER EIGHT:
Those Who Benefit From a Bullseye Marriage

The ritual of marriage is not simply a social event; it is a crossing of threads in the fabric of fate. Many strands bring the couple and their families together and spin their lives into a fabric that is woven on their children (and others). **Portuguese-Jewish Wedding Ceremony**

To have a "Bullseye Marriage" is a win-win relationship. There are no losers from a great marriage, only winners. According to research stated in the book, *The Case for Marriage*, by Linda J. Waite and Maggie Gallagher, couples who are happily married win by having healthier lives, both mentally and emotionally, than the unmarried, divorced, and widowed. Bullseye Marriages, where couples are intentionally targeting and investing time and energy in their marriages, are good for everyone.

1. *__Good for men and women__ – they live healthier life-styles, live longer live and have a more satisfying sexual relationship, greater wealth and economic assets.*

2. *__Good for children__ – better relationships with their parents; better relationships with peers; better emotional health; better success in school.*

3. *__Good for society__ – Strong marriages build strong families; strong families build strong schools, churches and neighborhoods that in turn builds strong civic communities and a strong nation.*

4. *__Good for business__ – Employees who are happily married are more loyal, stable and productive in their jobs. They live healthier lifestyles, take less time off from work, and have fewer health care expenditures than unmarried employees.*

5. *__Everyone wins when a marriage succeeds__ – People who invest in their marriages make the best parents, neighbors, PTA, church members, employees and citizens.*

   There are no perfect marriages, but there are successful marriages. And the difference between failure and success seems to be this: Successful couples work on their marriages.

__www. workonyourmarriage.org__

There is no perfect life, your life will be filled with successes and failures. It is your choice whether you live with regret because of the failures or choose to learn from the failures and celebrate the successes. The quality of your life experience depends on your ability to use the past as a school or as a club. Jim Rohn, a business philosopher, points out that you can take past hurts, failures, challenges and learn from this school of hard knocks to get better; self improve, and master your skills. Or you can use it as a club to destroy any chance of changing your future for a better life lived to the fullest.

As you focus your daily attention on becoming the best human being you can become, you actually do get better. Yes, you are not perfect and you will screw up and have to ask for forgiveness from those you hurt. The greater the pain the more time it will take to heal, but it all starts with the decision to seek and ask forgiveness. Or be the one to forgive.

Our children have been the closest to us these past twenty-four years of raising them. They have been witness to our successes and our failures. We asked them how they have benefited from observing our relationship. The following pages are their accounts of what they have witnessed and learned from our Bullseye Marriage.

Peter Joseph Fontana

(24 year old, married to Kristin Robbins Fontana and they have a 6-month-old, Audrey Therese)

As I stated in the foreword, my parents are not experts on marriage or marriage counselors. But they have become experts on each other. Because of their example, I can see the future for my wife and me if I practice the values of attaining a Bullseye Marriage.

The husband/father is such an essential element and yet a vastly abandoned role in today's society. Understanding what it means to be a husband/father is a key component to actually obtaining real manhood.

My father taught me that real manhood comes in taking responsibility for your actions and caring for those you love. I want to take the responsibility of taking care and pride in my family. I want to hold the responsibility of my wife's heart and love in my hands. I want to serve at the drop of a hat and take on the challenges that come with honor. I want to lead my family down the path and through the gates of heaven with my head held high and my family's colors flying high. These are the things that I have learned from my father. These are the things that he has inspired me to step into. He has called me into a greater manhood by simply taking ownership of the call he received from God and living it as husband to my mother and father to my siblings and me.

ON OUR 25ᵀᴴ ANNIVERSARY PETER WROTE THE
FOLLOWING LETTERS AND FRAMED THEM FOR US:

> **To Mom:** *Pope Paul VI talked about a "Civilization of Love" that combats the "Civilization of Death" that pervades our society. Pope John Paul II took that a step further in saying that the base unit of society is the family, the Domestic Church, in which the Civilization of Love needs to find its roots. If there was anyone who answered this call, it is you, Mom.*
>
> *You embraced your family as your primary mission grounds, and now the kids and I are the result of your "yes" to God in every aspect of our family life. You taught me that people are the priority and love the goal, and anything contrary to that should be reevaluated. As I reflect now, I begin to see for the first time the great sacrifices made just for our happiness. That in the business of our lifestyle, all of us accomplished what we set out*

to do because you were there to take us and rejoice in the triumphs and pick up the pieces of our failures.

You taught me that wrong is okay, but accepting the wrong is not. My most feared punishment was the hour long mandatory talk after whatever I did to "discuss" the validity and consequences of my actions. But now I find I am doing this with myself and mulling over how I would "do things differently" next time.

It was a long time before I accepted the greatest gift you gave and with much rebellion that I resisted it. This gift is the love you have for Dad. Your love for him does not seem to be a noun, it is not a thing, it is more of a verb. Your love is constantly moving, constantly growing and constantly acting.

You are a very independent woman, and in your independence you freely give yourself to Dad as he does to you, but it seems that you love without the expectation of a love returned but with rejoicing when it is returned.

It seems your identity flows from within yourself and your faith in Jesus Christ and includes your marriage in one flesh with Dad as a major proponent but not the thing that defines you. The beautiful thing as well is that you are also not defined by your children. I have found so much freedom from these truths, more than I will ever realize. It makes your choice to love and cherish Dad and us so much more dynamic and honoring.

I have realized of late that in searching for a wife and looking at the other women that I love and respect it is these qualities that I find in you that I search for. So here is congratulations for 25 years of freely given covenant love and commitment, of companionship ups and downs but centered on God and a son raised who is proud, blessed and honored to call you…Mom.

To Dad: You once gave me a shirt that said, "Give a man a fish and he will have dinner. Teach a man to fish and he will be late for dinner." Though this is a funny shirt, I believe this is how you have lived life. You would rather have done something with me than make something for me, and it was not until recently that I have seen the true value in that.

You taught me that the doing of a project is often more important that the project itself and that the gift of time and being fully present in that time is the greatest gift one can give another even if all the time you can spare is a quick basketball game or a nap on the living room floor.

I learned a lot of things from your direction, but the greatest things you taught me I have only begun to discover. They are the things that were lived and I truly believe, Dad, that your life lived will be the classroom of my living for years to come. You have truly embraced your Franciscan name and "preached the Gospel at all times," most especially with your actions. It is apparent in your relationships with everyone you meet, your kids, your colleagues and most especially with Mom.

This is the greatest gift you have given me and all of the kids, the daily practice of your cherishing love for Mom. I am honored to be a product of this love and a witness to it for the past twenty years. It is this masculine love, founded on the rock that is our Lord Jesus Christ, which shaped who I am today and my relationship with the world we live in, especially with Kristin.

When I was young I always sought your approval, it really was the key to my happiness. It is only now, after I have begun the journey of seeking to understand God as my Father, that I realize how much the father God gave me on earth already embraced this call. I never needed to seek your approval. You were constant in love that was not earned or weighed on a scale. Always inviting me to participate in your joy at my return and your joy in me being me. So congratulations on twenty five years of life well lived, love well loved, joy experienced and twenty years of a son raised who is proud, blessed and honored to call you…Dad.

(2018 update: Peter & Kristin now have 5 children. They live in Seabrook, Texas. Peter is a Missionary with Adore Ministries as Special Events Coordinator.)

Amelia Ruth Fontana

(21 year old, Senior at Texas A&M University, majoring in Education)

My parents' relationship has been a shining example in my life, and in the lives of my friends, of what a good, healthy, solid marriage looks like. Through their sacrificial love they have shown me what love is by the way that they give of themselves to each other and to us. Throughout the past 21 years I can remember my parents saying four main things about marriage: 1) Marriage is not easy; you have to work at it 2) Love is a choice. Each day I get up and choose to love your father (or mother) and you kids. 3) God first, spouse second, kids third and 4) Life is an adventure. It keeps getting better!

1) *"Marriage is not easy. You have to work at it."…Mom and Dad understood this statement from the very beginning. They knew that relationships in general took work, dedication, commitment, and time*

and marriage takes even more. But for as long as I can remember we have always been told that no matter what, we will never, NEVER have to worry about them getting a divorce. They are committed 100% to what they said on their wedding day and vows they took and nothing could change that. They make the choice each morning to continue working on their marriage. They continually work to keep God at the center of their relationship and their marriage. They understand the importance and value of romance and they will never let it die. We make jokes regularly in our family about how lovey-dovey Mom and Dad can be. The phrase, "Okay enough, your kids are still in the room!" is a pretty common one in our house. But it is not something that grosses me out (anymore, I might add). In fact, it is something that makes me proud. I'm proud to have parents who, after almost 30 years of marriage, are more in love today than they were on their wedding day. My dad makes it a point to tell us often (more often than we might like) how beautiful my mom is…and I love that about their relationship.

2) "Love is a choice. Each day I get up and choose to love your father (or mother) and you kids." Love is a choice. Love, by its very nature, requires sacrifice. Love can be difficult…it is not always easy to choose to do the dishes when you'd rather go to bed, but you do it out of love for your family. It is in those daily decisions that I see my parents' love for one another shine the most. My dad is a romantic! He loves to spoil my mom (and my sister and me); he takes the time to do the little things that mean so much to her. He takes the time to listen, to hold her, to do laundry, the dishes, the cooking and other house chores. He

takes the time to pick flowers for her and to tell her she's beautiful. He chooses to love her each day. And she chooses to love him as well. She chooses to let him go fishing, to help him in the yard, to go for walks with him, to help him cook and to allow him to love her. They make the choice to continue to love, and it is beautiful.

3) *"God first, spouse second, children third." This is the ranking of importance in our family. My parents have always taught us this. God comes first in all things. He is the source of our life; He is love. Your spouse comes second because they are your vocation or your calling in life. It is your job to help them get to heaven and to grow in holiness and in their relationship with God. Children come after the spouse, not before. That's the way it has always been in our family and the way it will be in my family, because it makes sense.*

4) *"Life is an adventure. It keeps getting better." No matter what unexpected difficulty life has thrown at our family, my parents have always maintained this belief…"Life keeps getting better!" Very rarely have I heard my parents talk about regrets because they live each moment to the fullest and live life with an enormous amount of JOY! My friends always know that my house is the party house— the Fontana's are always up for having people over because they enjoy the company, the games, the conversations and they laughter. They take each moment as it comes and live a life full of love, joy and happiness, and it is a great way to live!*

So how have I benefited from having parents with a healthy marriage? I have learned to live each moment to the fullest, to put God first in everything that I do and to wake up each morning and choose to love. I know that the man God has prepared for me will be someone like my dad—someone with a servant's heart, who knows what it means to love. My parents have shown me what I desire my marriage to one-day look like. I have learned the importance of communication at all times and about everything. I have learned the importance of laughter, romance, prayer and adventure just by watching them over the past 21 years. Their relationship has given me a sense of peace in knowing I will never have to go through the pain of watching my parents get divorced. Their relationship has shown me what true love looks like. The love that they have for one another mirrors the love that the Heavenly Father has for His Son. Their marriage is a sign, an icon, which points us to our Heavenly Father in the unique and beautiful way that marriage was created to. Their love is an inspiration and an example to so many people. I love having my friends meet my parents because their immediate response is, "Your parents are amazing!" You do not have to spend a lot of time with them to see that they are doing something right…. I am a product of their love, but their love reaches so many others because of its pure and holy intentions and the joy that it brings! I love you Mom and Dad and I couldn't be more proud to be your daughter!

(2018 update: Amelia married Vinny Chiara in 2014. They have 2 children and live in Houston. Amelia is teaches part time at St. Michaels Catholic School and enjoys the adventure of motherhood)

Evelyn Joy Fontana

(18 year old, freshman at Texas A&M University, majoring in dance/kinesiology)

The way you treat one another is so beautiful. It truly mirrors the way God calls a married couple to act in the Bible. You treat each other with such respect and with total selflessness. I know that when I'm discerning to date a guy, I ask myself, "Does he treat me the way my father does?" Watching Dad with Mom makes me feel so blessed to know that I have parents who love one another and keep Christ at the center of everything. They have set a beautiful example of what a free, total, faithful, and fruitful relationship looks like. It is a gift to me beyond words, and I am so grateful.

Today in our society we have so many divorces. Some statistics state as much as 50% of all marriages end in divorce. Many of my friends come from parents who are divorced. Despite these facts all around me, I have had the benefit of observing the way Mom and Dad work together, respond to one another, and share the responsibility of raising the four of us. One of the big blessings I have today is the confidence that two people can be married to the same person for a lifetime. I have seen from my parents and grandparents that marriage works for those who work on their marriages.

Many of my friends have told me how blessed I am to have a family that loves each other and supports one another. I have seen the hurt and pain some of my friends have gone through when their parents went through divorce. Their sense of security was shattered. I know that marriage can work because I have witnessed my parents go through good times and bad times, experience abundant times financially and go through difficult times with money issues. Throughout the good and the bad, they worked hard to maintain good communication and attitudes. They have taught me to choose the right attitude in any given situation, especially when the times are not to my liking and most challenging.

Having a good marriage has a rippling effect. Having had the privilege of observing Mom and Dad's relationship has made me see what a truly loving relationship embodies. Peter and Kristin got married with a very good understanding of what it takes to hit the Bullseye of a marriage. This rippling effect has been a blessing to me, because I have been able to not only see my parents' relationship, but also my brother's relationship and how he has made this thought process his own. Although I have not always understood this, I am so grateful that my parents have always made it very clear that in their lives they strive to put God first, their spouse second, and us kids third.

(2018 update: Evelyn Joy married James Hoelscher in 2015. They live in New York City. Evelyn Joy is a professional dancer and has started her own dance company. You can follow her at www.spacesoffontana.com)

Michael Francis Fontana

(17 year old, Junior at Clear Creek High School)

Being the youngest, I have had the benefit and the misfortune of seeing Mom and Dad's relationship and parenting grow after many years of raising my older siblings. I say misfortune because, by the time I went into high school and began driving, my parents learned from my brother and sisters of what to do and what not to do. I've come to appreciate them for this, although it does get annoying at times. The benefits, however, are much greater than the misfortune. For example, my older two siblings, Peter and

Amelia, are always saying that I get more stuff than they did, yet they got away with more. But more than that, I've had the chance to observe my parents grow in their relationship. I've observed that when my dad gets that glow in his eyes and starts working on another big project that my mother will let him go have his fun and bring a cup of water to him or just go and watch him work. And when my mom goes on her long never-ending rant about the world and how she's going to fix it, he will listen with a smile and love. Although they both may not like what the other is doing, they still will be there and support the other.

Since I am still growing and learning more about the world I really have observed my dad and the way he treats and loves my mom. Watching my dad love my mom has shown me that love has a lot to do with being willing to serve. This has taught me that I must be willing to be a servant to my future wife for a marriage to be successful. I believe also that this willingness to serve must come from both sides—the man and the wife. Both of my parents have learned to serve each other fully and unselfishly. They are not perfect— and they struggle— but they work hard at it and learn from each other.

My parents and their marriage has always been about being positive and finding the good in every situation. As annoying as this was to always have this in my ear, they taught me to accept responsibility for my own actions and not blame others for the things that don't go my way. I have learned this is especially true in marriages especially to not blame one another for problems and to not make excuses if something doesn't go your way. Challenges will happen and, although I get very frustrated at times and would like to blame other people, I have learned from my parents to *accept my own responsibility for what happens.*

(2018 update: Michael graduated from Benedictine College in 2017. He works with St. Paul's Outreach and is currently assigned to Texas State University in San Marcos, Texas as a Catholic Campus Minister.)

Our kids give a great report on how they have benefited from our working on our marriage. If you sat down with them, they could also tell you about the days when we did not hit the target, much less the Bullseye. What they learned from those days is that, when we argued, or got frustrated with one another, it did not mean that we were going to throw in the bow and never strive for the Bullseye again. What they learned is that we were committed 100% to working on our marriage. They learned it is not easy, but it is worth it. There will be good days, bad days, average days and great days. It's all part of the process of developing the skills to hit the Bullseye.

We had that same benefit from watching our own parents as they worked on their marriages. We went into our marriage with the extra benefit that both of us came from families where the parents had been committed to working on their relationships. When you don't have that in your own life, it is important to look around and find examples of couples who exhibit what you want in your marriage. Seek marriage counseling and coaching from someone who believes in marriage and can help you develop your Clear Concise Mental Picture of a good relationship and then help you develop the skills to achieve that picture. Skills have to be learned and practiced. A bullseye at the archery range does not just happen. The archer has to learn the skills and keep practicing. In the same way, a Bullseye Marriage does not just happen. You, have to develop and then communicate with one another the target you are shooting for, learn the skills to hit the target, and keep practicing on a daily basis. It is worth it, not only for you as a couple but also for all those whose lives you touch!

Kristin Robbins Fontana

(24 years old, married Peter Fontana on April 18, 2009.)

We have had the privilege and honor of welcoming a daughter-in-law into our family. Kristin Robbins Fontana has been a part of our life for many years now and we are grateful that she took a moment to describe how our marriage has benefited her as she and our son, Peter, work on creating their own Bullseye Marriage:

I first met Sara and Francis when I knocked on their door to pick up their oldest son. Peter agreed to come as my date to the homecoming game of our freshman year of high school. I was greatly intimidated by the interest they had in our plans and the fact that Peter had to get their permission to do just about everything.

I did not really have a high opinion of marriage at the time. My parents divorced when I was 12 and I thereafter was raised with separated parents who loved me, but employed little "parenting," so to speak. There were no curfews or inquiries into where I was going, why I was going there, who was going to be there, or when I would be back (all questions I was appalled to find out Peter's mom needed to have answered before he could do anything!). So needless to say I was very much curious about this extremely odd concept of parents needing to know every infinitesimal detail about the goings-on of their children!

My curiosity in their parenting techniques led to fascination and eventually to admiration as Peter's and my relationship grew into a long term courtship. As I investigated these parenting techniques that I admired so much, my observation led me to realize that the root and foundation of Sara and Francis' parenting was their relationship with each other. I began to see that it was this relationship, after their individual relationships with God, which took utmost priority, even before the family matters. This was truly a shock to me. I had never before made any connection between parenting and the relationship between the parents. Upon realizing the significance of the husband-wife relationship, I then began to investigate more into what made Francis and Sara's relationship different.

The phrase, "You complete me," was one I always associated with finding a marital partner. I thought I needed someone to complete me and make me whole (as if I was ever "half" a person!). However, Sara and Francis demonstrated something else. They showed me that a marriage that hits the bullseye more often than not involves each partner knowing themselves, and being complete on their own and with God. Before I found love I needed to find myself. I needed to be myself, my own individual. Both Sara and Francis are unique individuals. They have their own unique traits, ideas, personalities, and philosophies. Together they complement one another equally without giving or taking too much from one another and thus are one entity. I have learned that marriage is not 50/50 it's 100/100—husband and wife both giving 100 percent of themselves 100 percent of the time. Sara and Francis are themselves and they have taught their children to be the same way. Thus, having married their oldest son, I have quite a rock in my life.

The transition after marrying Peter and experiencing a change from admiring girlfriend to daughter-in-law and matron of my own family uncovered a new lesson. As much as I thought I wanted to exactly reproduce their marriage so that our kids would turn out like theirs, I started realizing that Peter's and my Bullseye was different than Sara and Francis'. I realized that we could not model their marriage exactly. We had to create and shoot for our own Bullseye, and I would like to think that Peter and I have learned how to hit our Bullseye more than miss it in our young marriage. We get to take the lessons of the Fontanas' and build on them.

(2018 update: Kristin serves alongside Peter as a Missionary with Adore Ministries with her main focus being dedicated to being a mother of their 5 children.)

CHAPTER NINE:

Resources

What we have been promised is greater than we can imagine. May we never lose heart because of our limitations, or ever stop seeking that fullness of love and communion which God holds out before us.

Pope Francis in The Joy of Love

SUGGESTED BOOKS

The Joy of Love by Pope Francis

The Four Seasons of Marriage by Gary Chapman

The Five Love Languages by Gary Chapman

Anger: Handling a Powerful Emotion in a Healthy Way by Gary Chapman

Desperate Marriages: Moving Toward Hope and Healing in Your Marriage by Gary Chapman

Everybody Wins: The Chapman Guide to Solving Conflicts Without Arguing by Gary Chapman

Now You're Speaking My Language by Gary Chapman

Making Love: The Chapman Guide to Making Sex an Act of Love by Gary Chapman

Good Marriages Don't Just Happen by Catherine & Joseph Garcia-Prats

Heaven's Song: Sexual Love as It Was Meant to Be by Christopher West

The Good News About Sex and Marriage by Christopher West

Theology of the Body for Beginners by Christopher West

Man and Woman He Created Them: Theology of the Body by Pope John Paul II Translated by Michael Waldstein

Love and Responsibility by Pope John Paul II

Holy Sex by Gregory K. Popcak, Ph.D.

The Four Loves by C.S. Lewis

Hidden Keys of a Loving Lasting Relationship by Gary & Norma Smalley

Love is a Decision by Gary Smalley and John Trent

Please Understand Me II by David Keirsey

Mapping the Mind by Rita Carter

Laugh Your Way to a Better Marriage By Mark Gungor

The Five Major Pieces of the Life Puzzle by Jim Rohn

Follow the Way of Love: A Pastoral Message of the U.S. Catholic Bishops to Families. 1994 United States Catholic Conference, Inc. Washington, D.C.

The Case for Marriage by Linda J. Waite and Maggie Gallagher

Deus Caritas Est (God is Love) Encyclical, Pope Benedict XVI

When Bad Things Happen to Good Marriages By Drs. Les & Leslie Parrott

St. George and the Dragon and the Quest for the Holy Grail by Edward Hays

Doors to the Sacred by Joseph Martos

The Two Sides of Love by Gary Smalley and John Trent, Ph.D.

Intended For Pleasure by Ed Wheat, M.D. and Gaye Wheat

A Lasting Promise: A Christian Guide To Fighting For Your Marriage by Scott Stanley, Daniel Trathen, Savanna McCain, Milt Bryan

10 Great Dates to Energize Your Marriage by David & Claudia Arp

The Noticer by Andy Andrews

The Joy of Love by Pope Francis

Familiaris Consortio Pope John Paul II

SUGGESTED INTERNET SITES...
FOR INTENTIONALLY TARGETING A GREAT RELATIONSHIP....

www.workonyourmarriage.com Great articles by Dr. Robert Fontana - some quite humorous but all terrific ideas which support Robert & Lori Fontana's idea "that your marriage works when you work on your marriage." Also provides marriage coaching and seminars.

www.foryourmarriage.com this is a great website that the marriage and family life office of the United States Conference of Catholic Bishops put together. Wonderful articles and ideas from various authors.

www.divorcebusting.com Awesome ideas and content for working on your marriage. Developed by marriage counselor Michele Weiner-Davis.

www.smartmarriages.com This website is put together by a group which puts together Smart Marriage conferences. Multiple authors with great ideas.

www.susanvogt.net This is a colleague whom Sara has worked with through the years. Again some good ideas brought forth from her many years of marriage.

www.marriagebuilders.com Website developed by Dr. Willard F. Harley, Jr. Has variety of excellent Questionnaires to help you get in touch with your needs and assist in communicating. Also offers marriage coaching.

www.marriagemap.com Rob and Tess Davis have put together a terrific website and program that is specifically addressed to wives. You can sign up for the Marriage Map – 90 days to a Spectacular Marriage. They send short videos and coach you on skills to achieve a spectacular marriage.

www.laughyourway.com website for Mark Gungor. Offers Better Marriage Minutes heard on radios as well as marriage seminars. You can locate some of Mark Gungor's presentations on YouTube.

www.garychapman.com Official website of Dr. Gary Chapman author of *The Five Love Languages*. Provides a "Love Language" Assessment to help you determine your love language.

FOR PERSONALITY PROFILES AND GETTING TO KNOW YOURSELF BETTER...

www.keirsey.com Personality test using the official Keirsey Temperament Sorter.

www.myersbriggs.org Official website for the Myers-Briggs Personality Profile.

www.personalitytype.com Quick assessment of your Myers-Briggs Personality type.

www.true-colors.com Personality profile using colors.

www.smalley.cc Official website for Dr. Gary Smalley and his family. Has Personality Tests as well as Healthy Marriage tests. Also has articles about the 5 love languages.

FOR TOWER TIME GET AWAYS AND FOR WHEN YOU ARE HURTING...

www.clearingretreat.org Marriage Intensive Retreats done in beautiful settings and "Good to Great" Marriage Enrichment Workshops. Also has a phone number to call for couples in crisis.

www.retrouvaille.org Retrouvaille is a French word which means rediscovery. Retrouvaille is a retreat that helps couples heal and renew their marriages. It offers tools needed to rediscover a loving marriage relationship

www.loveyourelationship.com offers couples retreats, relationship coaching and Prevention and Relationship Enhancement Program (PREP). With Dr. Howard Markman.

www.marriagemax.com With Mort Fertel. Offers Marriage Fitness System for relationship renewal.

www.circlelakeretreat.org A place to get away as a couple for quiet and reconnecting or come with your whole family. Book a house and take some time to enjoy the gardens or just sitting in the rocking chair on your porch and watching the swans in the lake. Take the time for recreation, relaxing and enjoying natural beauty.

SUGGESTED CATECHISMS
OF THE CATHOLIC CHURCH

(Taken from *Catechism of the Catholic Church*, published by Doubleday, 1995)

Specific paragraphs concerning marriage:

#1604 God who created man out of love also calls him to love – the fundamental and innate vocation of every human being. For man is created in the image and likeness of God who is himself love. Since God created him man and woman, their mutual love becomes an image of the absolute and unfailing love with which God loves man. It is good, very good, in the Creator's eyes. And this love which God blesses is intended to be fruitful and to be realized in the common work of watching over creation: "And God blessed them, and God said to them: 'Be fruitful and multiply, and fill the earth and subdue it.'"

#1605 Holy Scripture affirms that man and woman were created for one another: "It is not good that the man should be alone." The woman, "flesh of his flesh," his equal, his nearest in all things, is given to him by God as a "helpmate"; she thus represents God from whom comes our help. "Therefore a man leaves his father and his mother and cleaves to his wife, and they become one flesh." The Lord himself shows that this signifies an unbreakable union of their two lives by recalling what the plan of the Creator had been "in the beginning": "So the are no longer two, but one flesh."

#1613 On the threshold of his public life Jesus performs his first sign – at his mother's request – during a wedding feast. The Church attaches great importance to Jesus' presence at the wedding at Cana. She sees in it the confirmation of the goodness of marriage and the proclamation that thenceforth marriage will be an efficacious sign of Christ's presence.

#1614 In his preaching Jesus unequivocally taught the original meaning of the union of man and woman as the Creator willed it from the beginning: permission given by Moses to divorce one's wife was a concession to the hardness of hearts. The matrimonial union of man and woman is indissoluble: God himself has determined it: "what therefore God has joined together, let no man put asunder."

#1615 The unequivocal insistence on the indissolubility of the marriage bond may have left some perplexed and could seem to be a demand impossible to realize. However, Jesus has not placed on spouses a burden impossible to bear, or too heavy – heavier than the Law of Moses. By coming to restore the original order of creation disturbed by sin, he himself gives the strength and the grace to live marriage in the new dimension of the Reign of God. It is by following Christ, renouncing themselves, and taking up their crosses that spouses will be able to "receive" the original meaning of marriage and live it with the help of Christ. This grace of Christian marriage is a fruit of Christ's cross, the source of all Christian life.

#1616 This is what the Apostle Paul makes clear when he says: "Husbands, love your wives, as Christ loved the church and gave himself up for her, that he might sanctify her,; adding at once: "For this reason a man shall leave his father and mother and be joined to his wife, and the tow shall becomes one. This is a great mystery, and I mean in reference to Christ and the Church."

#1617 The entire Christian life bears the mark of the spousal love of Christ and the Church. Already Baptism, the entry into the People of God, is a nuptial mystery; it is so to speak the nuptial bath which precedes the wedding feast, the Eucharist. Christian marriage in its turn becomes an efficacious sign, the sacrament of the covenant of Christ and the Church. Since it signifies and communicates great, marriage between baptized persons is a true sacrament of the New Covenant.

#1621 In the Latin Rite the celebration of marriage between two Catholic faithful normally takes place during Holy Mass, because of the connection of all the sacraments with the Paschal mystery of Christ. In the Eucharist the memorial of the New Covenant is realized, the New Covenant in which Christ has united himself for ever to the Church, his beloved bride for whom he gave himself up. It is therefore fitting that the spouses should seal their consent to give themselves to each other through the offering of their own lives by uniting it to the offering of Christ for his Church made present in the Eucharistic sacrifice, and by receiving the Eucharist so that, communicating in the same Body and the same Blood of Christ, they may form but "one body" in Christ.

#1624 The various liturgies abound in prayers of blessing and epiclesis asking God's grace and blessing on the new couple, especially the bride. In the epiclesis of this sacrament the spouses receive the Holy Spirit as the

communion of love of Christ and the Church. The Holy Spirit is the seal of their covenant, the ever-available source of their love and the strength to renew their fidelity.

#1625 The parties to a marriage covenant are a baptized man and woman, free to contract marriage, who freely express their consent; "to be free" means:

> ➢ *Not being under constraint;*

> ➢ *Not impeded by any natural or ecclesiastical law.*

#1626 The Church holds the exchange of consent between the spouses to be the indispensable element that "makes the marriage." If consent is lacking there is no marriage.

#1627 The consent consist in a "human act by which the partners mutually give themselves to each other": "I take you to be my wife" – "I take you to be my husband." This consent that binds the spouses to each other finds its fulfillment in the two "becoming one flesh."

#1628 The consent must be an act of the will of each of the contracting parties, free of coercion or grave external fear. No human power can substitute for this consent If this freedom is lacking the marriage is invalid.

#1631 This is the reason why the Church normally requires that the faithful contract marriage according to the ecclesiastical form. Several reasons converge to explain this requirement.

> ➢ *Sacramental marriage is a liturgical act. It is therefore appropriate that it should be celebrated in the public liturgy of the Church;*

> ➢ *Marriage introduces one into an ecclesial order, and creates rights and duties in the Church between the spouses and towards their children;*

> ➢ *Since marriage is a state of life in the Church, certainty about it is necessary (hence the obligation to have witnesses);*

> ➢ *The public character of the consent protects the "I do" once given and helps the spouses remain faithful to it.*

#1632 So that the "I do" of the spouses may be a free and responsible act and so that the marriage covenant may have solid and lasting human and Christian foundations, preparation for marriage is of prime importance.

The example and teaching given by parents and families remain the special form of this preparation.

The role of pastors and of the Christian community as the "family of God" is indispensable for the transmission of the human and Christian values of marriage and family, and much more so in our era when many young people experience broken homes which no longer sufficiently assure their initiation:

> *It is imperative to give suitable and timely instruction to young people, above all in the heart of their own families, about the dignity of married love, its role and its exercise, so that, having learned the value of chastity, they will be able at a suitable age to engage in honorable courtship and enter upon a marriage of their own.*

#1638 "From a valid marriage arises a bond between the spouses which by its very nature is perpetual and exclusive; furthermore, in a Christian marriage the spouses are strengthened and, as it were, consecrated for the duties and the dignity of their state by a special sacrament."

#1639 The consent by which the spouses mutually give and receive one another is sealed by God himself. From their covenant arises "an institution, confirmed by the divine law,...even in the eyes of society." The covenant between the spouses is integrated into God's covenant with man: "Authentic married love is caught up into divine love."

#1640 Thus the marriage bond has been established by God himself in such a way that a marriage concluded and consummated between baptized persons can never be dissolved. This bond, which results from the free human act of the spouses and their consummation of the marriage, is a reality, henceforth irrevocable, and gives rise to a covenant guaranteed by God's fidelity. The Church does not have the power to contravene this disposition of divine wisdom.

#1643 "Conjugal love involves a totality, in which all the elements of the person enter – appeal of the body and instinct, power of feeling and affectivity, aspiration of the spirit and of will. It aims at a deeply personal unity, a unity that, beyond union in one flesh, leads to forming one heart and soul; it demands indissolubility and faithfulness in definitive mutual

giving; and it is open to fertility. In a word it is a question of the normal characteristics of all natural conjugal love, but with a new significance which not only purifies and strengthens them, but raises them to the extent of making them the expression of specifically Christian values."

#1644 The love of the spouses requires, of its very nature, the unity and indissolubility of the spouses' community of person, which embraces their entire life: "so they are no longer two, but one flesh." They are called to grow continually in their communion through day—to-day fidelity to their marriage promise of total mutual self-giving." This human communion is confirmed, purified, and completed by communion in Jesus Christ, given through the sacrament of Matrimony. It is deepened by lives of the common faith and by the Eucharist received together.

#1646 By it very nature conjugal love requires the inviolable fidelity of the spouses. This is the consequence of the gift of themselves which they make to each other. Love seeks to be definitive; it cannot be an arrangement "until further notice." The "intimate union of marriage, as a mutual giving of two persons, and the good of the children, demand total fidelity from the spouses and require an unbreakable union between them."

#1648 It can seem difficult, even impossible, to bind oneself for life to another human being. This makes it all the more important to proclaim the Good News that God loves us with a definitive and irrevocable love, that married couples share in this love, that it supports and sustains them, and that by their own faithfulness they can be witnesses to God's faithful love. Spouses, who with God's grace give this witness, often in very difficult conditions, deserve the gratitude and support of the ecclesial community.

HISTORY OF MARRIAGE IN A COUPLE OF NUTSHELLS

(Compiled from *New American Bible* and

Open the Doors to the Sacred, by Joseph Martos)

ANCIENT NUTSHELL

1ˢᵀ Century – In Jesus' words. Actually there are very few words that Jesus spoke on marriage that are recorded in the Bible. He used marriage & wedding feasts in parables (Matthew 22:1-14, Matthew 25:1-13, Luke 14:12-24). He attended the wedding at Cana. (John 2:11) And he answered questions about marriage and divorce. One question, posed to him by the Sadducees, concerned the state of marriage after one dies (Matthew 22:23-33, Mark 12:18-27, Luke 20:34-39). Jesus' response was, "When people rise from the dead, they neither marry nor are given in marriage but live as angels in heaven." In other words, we are married until "death do us part."

The other question concerned divorce (Matthew 19:3-12, Mark 10:2-12, Luke 16:18). Some Pharisees asked, "May a man divorce his wife for any reason whatever?" Jesus replied, "Have you not heard that at the beginning the Creator made them male and female and declared that 'for this reason a man shall leave his father and mother and cling to his wife, and the two shall become as one'? Thus, they are no longer two but one flesh. Therefore, let no man separate what God has joined." Jesus declares the scriptural doctrine he quotes from Genesis to be God's ultimate intent for marriage in human society, explaining that the divorce granted in Mosaic law was due to the stubbornness of the people.

In Epistles: The Epistles are rich with descriptions on how we are to live as followers of Christ. There are a just a few specific ones that address how to do this in marriage:

In Ephesians 5: 22-33, Paul provides the notion that marriage and the relationship between a husband and wife is a reflection of Christ's relationship with the Church. The wife symbolizes the Church. The Church should be submissive to Christ and respectful of Christ's position as head of it. The husband symbolizes Christ and he is called to love his wife as Christ loved the Church. A tall order is given to husbands as Paul exhorts them to "give yourself up for her...love your wife as you love your own body...nourish her and take care of her as Christ takes care of the Church."

4th Century - Marriage was primarily a family and secular affair with the bride's father playing the chief role in the wedding ceremony. There were no official words that had to be spoken, and there was no church blessing that had to be given to make the marriage legal and binding.

5th Century - the wedding ceremony developed into a liturgical action in which the priest joined the couple in marriage and blessed their union, but still this ceremony was not mandatory and through the seventh century Christians could still get married in a purely secular ceremony. Augustine confirmed marriage was a visible sign of the invisible union between Christ and his spouse, the church. Christian marriage was a sacred pledge of fidelity. He affirmed marriage was good, but the sole purpose of the sexual act should be to have children. Sexual desire according to Augustine was a dangerous, destructive force.

8th Century - Liturgy weddings had become quite common and they were usually performed in a church rather than in a home as before. In the Greek Church marriage became an ecclesial ceremony and a priest's blessing was essential for the joining of two people in a Christian marriage.

MIDDLE AGE NUTSHELL

9th Century- in 802 Charlemagne passed a law requiring all proposed marriages to be examined for legal restrictions before the wedding could take place.

11th Century - Became customary to hold the wedding near a church so that the newly married couple could go inside immediately afterward to obtain the priest's blessing.

12th Century - Pope Alexander III decreed that the consent given by the two partners was all that was needed for the existence of a real marriage. From the moment of consent a true marriage contract took place The sexual intercourse was thought to complete or consummate the marriage only – it was not needed for the marriage to actually take place. Marriage became recognized as one of the Church's official Sacraments.

13th Century - Thomas Aquinas stated that the sacramental reality of the marriage bond which was created by consent and made permanent through consummation was permanent. As a natural institution marriage was ordered for the good of nature, the perpetuation of the human race and was regulated by natural laws which resulted in the birth of children. As a social institution it was ordered to the good of society, the perpetuation of the family, and the state and was regulated by civil laws which governed the political, social and economic responsibilities of married persons. As a sacrament, it was ordered to the good of the Church, the perpetuation of the community of those who loved, worshipped and obeyed the one true God, and was regulated by the divine laws which governed the reception of grace and growth in spiritual perfection.

15th Century - Council of Florence 1439 – Marriage was listed as one of the 7 sacraments of the Roman church and explained as a sign of the union between Christ and the Church

16th Century - Protestant Era began. In 1520, Martin Luther stated in his treatise *Babylonian Captivity of the Church,* "Since marriage existed since the beginning of the world and is still found among unbelievers, it cannot possible be called a sacrament of the New Law and the exclusive property of the Church." During that time period, Luther wrote several treatises regarding marriage. In 1563 at the Council of Trent the Roman church responded to the reformers statements on marriage. The bishops affirmed that God had made the bond of marriage unbreakable when he made the first man and woman and that Christ had both reaffirmed this and made marriage a sacrament. They also established the form that the couple is to be married before a priest and two or three witnesses.

17th Century - the beginning of the Protestant era and through the 17th Century other Christian churches developed their own wedding ceremonies. For most of this century almost all marriages in Europe were church marriages.

18th Century - French Revolution and other political upheavals brought an end to church control of marriage. In fact the Napoleonic Code of 1792 made civil weddings mandatory for all French citizens. People could then marry before a civil magistrate instead of a priest or minister.

MODERN NUTSHELL

19th Century - In 1880 Pope Leo XIII stated in his encyclical, Arcanum *divinae spaieantiae,* that "Christian marriage cannot be separated from the sacrament, and for this reason the contract cannot be a true and lawful one without being a sacrament as well." Questions began to arise in the Catholic Church from around the world that were sent to canon lawyers to answer. "Were marriages between Christians and non-Christians sacramental as well?" Could a legally divorced non-Catholic validly marry a single Catholic?" Cases were sent to Rome and to canon lawyers, and the decisions made set precedents for future cases.

20th Century - The nature and function of marriage in the West began to change. Before it was a social duty; now it was an individual right. Before it was done in compliance with parents' wishes; now it was done for personal love. Before, love was expected to begin after the wedding; now it was expected to precede it. There were parallel changes in the nature and function of the family. Before, the family was the basic unit of society: families lived and worked together; children were educated, trades were learned, recreation was provided and most human needs were met, all within and by the family. Now, the family was becoming but one social unit among many: people had jobs that took them away from the people they lived with, children went to schools, most occupations could no longer be learned from one's parents, recreation was brought in by printed or electronic media or sought outside the home and most human needs except the most basic ones of nurturing and affection were met by people outside the family. In short, marriage was coming to be seen mainly as an expression of love between a man and a woman. The Catholic Church addressed marriage in various documents:

- o 1962 the Vatican II documents
- o 1968 Encyclical by Pope Paul VI entitled
  - Humanae Vitae (of Human Life)
- o 1981 Familiaris Consortio (On the Family) Encyclical Letter by Pope John Paul II
- o 1992 Catechism of the Catholic Church
- o 1997 Daughters of St. Paul compiled Pope John Paul II weekly audience presentations given from 1979 – 1984 and titled the book THEOLOGY OF THE BODY

21st Century - In the United States the state governments grant the marriage license and clergy are legally qualified to perform the wedding and sign the documents. The states however determine who can and who cannot get a license for marriage Most churches now have a preparation time and some sort of couple counseling that is required before the wedding can take place in their churches.

INDEX

To schedule a Bullseye Marriage Conference or
presentation contact Sara Fontana at
Bullseyemarriage@yahoo.com

To order more copies of this book and connect

to other marriage resources go to our website:

www.bullseyemarriage.com